PIECE OF MIND

Science today has shown us how we can access all our
mind in seconds — it's like turning on a switch
inside your mind.

With the information in this book you can not only
Switch On to all of your mind in seconds, you can increase
the use of your mind to achieve faster and more easily.

Switch On to your personal power.

PIECE OF MIND

Sandy MacGregor

Mind Charts

by

Monika Kobus

First published in Australia March 1992
Reprints: June, August, October 1992
February, May, October, December 1993
August 1994 and November 1995
Revised and reprinted in Australia in July 1996

Published by

CALM PTY LTD (ACN 060 570 818)
2nd Level, 80 Chandos Street, Crows Nest NSW 2065, Australia.
PO Box 482, Lindfield NSW 2070, Australia.
Telephone: (02) 439 7188 Facsimile: (02) 439 7587

E Mail — calm@ozemail.com.au
Internet Home Page — www.lightenup.com.au/calm

Printed and Bound by
Southwood Press Pty Limited
80-92 Chapel Street, Marrickville, NSW, 2204

Distributed in Australia by
Capricorn Link (Australia) Pty Ltd
2/13 Carrington Road, Castle Hill, NSW 2154

Tapes and Videos Distributed in Australia by
Quest Pty Limited
Theosophy House, 484 Kent Street, Sydney, NSW 2000

Distributed in New Zealand by
Tandem Press
Rugby Road, Birkenhead, Auckland 10

ISBN 0 646 08455 0

DEDICATION

I dedicate this book to my three children who can no longer be here with me in body, but always will be in spirit: Jenny, Kirsty and Lexie. It has been what I have learned from their untimely death and the direction I have moved in since their death that has driven me and been my inspiration.

I also dedicate my book to my three children who live on with me in both body and spirit: Andrew, Lara and Ian. They have also been my inspiration and it is through them that I continue to learn and know that whatever happens life moves on and on ....

ACKNOWLEDGEMENTS

I thank my wife Sandra for the long hours, patience and support she's given me whilst we both worked on this book. Sandra does many things to constantly make life run smoothly in addition to being a wonderful mother.

Thank you to Monika Kobus, for the wonderful artwork; it has been a delight to work with Monika. I would also like to thank Susan St Lawrence and Victor Wilson who have so capably assisted with the running of my seminars.

Steven Snyder is a friend who instructed me so well at Insight IV. I thank him for his friendship, for his encouragement and for his wonderfully clear teaching style.

To Ken Davis a big thank you for his assistance and encouragement and for the marvellous piece of music he has composed for me: *Infinite Joy*.

I highly recommend Insight Seminars as a wonderful personal awareness organisation which had a great influence on me.

Many others, too numerous to list, have helped me along the way and I thank you all: you know who you are.

Finally, I would like to acknowledge myself and say; "Well done Sandy!" I hope this book may also inspire you and contribute to your life's purpose.

CONTENTS

FOREWORD

Is there any new information under the sun? The human race places its own limitations on belief — we want everything to be proven to us scientifically. Recently (in the last 30 years) an enormous amount of research has been accomplished in the field of learning and particularly the brain, which researchers, scientists and psychologists have been able to label with new words — the "new" discoveries. This makes it more acceptable to us. Has accelerated learning, (ie. the ability to achieve faster, both academically and gain life skills) using relaxation and the power of the subconscious mind, always been with man? The answer is YES. Many great artists, scientists and inventors have used it, but it was not labelled "accelerated learning". All of us have used it — especially between the ages of 0 to 5. (Scientists now tell us this, so we have come to accept it).

This book is about **how to use the subconscious** mind to our own advantage. The subconscious mind is 88% power of our mind. It is a storehouse for memory — all memory — including habits. You use this mind effectively only in the relaxed state; the language of the subconscious mind is emotion. So what does this book do differently? It teaches **how to relax in 30 seconds and how to use emotion**; the two most important tools towards achieving accelerated learning — not only academic learning, but life skills learning (increasing confidence, releasing weight, enhancing artistic abilities, releasing stress, increasing sales, sleeping easily, etc, etc). We have all heard of mind power courses — this book uses plain language to "take the mystery out of mind power", making it available to all those who seek it. We all use mind power — but we can use it more and it's our *right* to know about it!

In presenting the information, I have used three major resources: the first — myself and my experiences. References for scientific research can be found in Colin Rose's book *Accelerated Learning* — basically it summarises the research available in this field. My third major resource is my association with Steven Snyder — his clear, explicit language and lucid explanations are really worth emulating.

I am motivated by my belief in these methods, this "mind power", which has been of such tremendous benefit to me. I would like to share this with as many people as possible. I conduct my seminars, and I love doing that, however I know that with this book I will reach an even wider audience, and that would please me greatly. So who is this book for? We are all at different phases or stages in our lives. This book can be for taking control of our individual power, it can be the start of charting a new direction, it can be for parents wishing to impart skills to their children, it can be for those who wish to relax and release stress, it can be for those who wish to change or reinforce a habit or to increase self confidence and self esteem, it can be for those who wish to learn faster with no stress involved, it can be for those who wish to know about the skills of academic learning, it can be for those taking the first step to meditation, it can be for busy professional people to make more time in their lives, it can be for corporations applying the skills to increase sales, for motivation, etc. Have I missed anyone? I hope not.

HOW TO USE THIS BOOK

To gain an overview, look at the Mind Charts at the beginning of each chapter and then at the end of each chapter. Your next step is to read each chapter and complete the exercises as you go.

Questions raised in telephone conversations and in discussion sessions are included. If you have more please write to me. Read the personal stories, they show many examples of how these techniques have worked for various achievements.

On completion, review this book by looking at the Mind Charts at the end of each chapter.

The audio tapes *A Peaceful Place (PP) No.1 (Instrumental)* and *A PP No.2 (Guided Imagery)* are available (see page 230) or you could make your own guided imagery tapes using the written words (where indicated in italics) in this book.

With the tapes and this book you can achieve relaxation in thirty seconds; you can apply this to academic learning, by experiencing new techniques. By creating and using your Emotional Anchor, you will be able to use these techniques to program goals and achieve them faster.

Practise the Alpha technique 20 times a day for a month — each practice is 30 seconds so that's 10 minutes a day to help you create the best possible habit you can have. A habit that saves you time, focuses your energy and helps you achieve anything you want — faster. **Remember, doing it does it.**

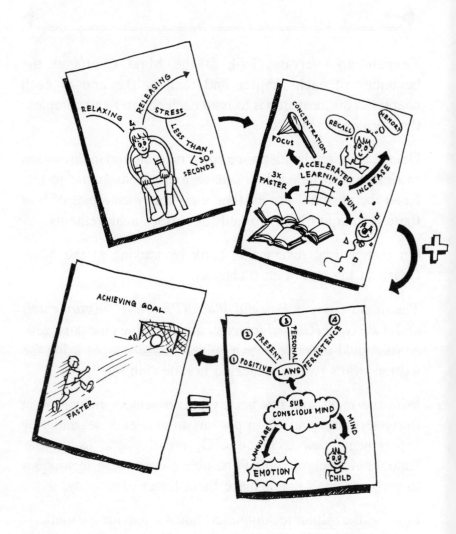

PREVIEW OF WHAT THIS BOOK IS ABOUT

1

INTRODUCTION

I was introduced to the subject of the powers we have within us by my son Andrew, when he was 17 years old, in 1982. It happened like this. Andrew at that stage had been suffering from asthma for about 15 years, and he actually collapsed at a railway station, was taken to a hospital, and given a cortisone drip. He woke up attached to a drip, which he pulled out of his arm, walked out of the hospital, collapsed again, and ended up in another hospital on another cortisone drip. In fact he rang me from the second hospital — I didn't know anything about what had happened until his call. Up until that stage of course he had received so much conventional treatment for asthma and was not achieving any relief or recovery, so I decided to seek some alternative treatment.

I introduced him to a doctor who actually taught Andrew how to relax between bouts of asthma — this was quite fantastic. The treatment started to work — Andrew was taking control. A few months later, Andrew had an argument with a bus; he was on a motor bike, and he lost. The result was that his leg was broken in two places. He did a really good job on himself, with bones sticking out — crushed and shattered — but he never lost consciousness. Andrew actually had the control and the ability, some power within him, that enabled him to go to that "place of relaxation" that the doctor had taught him about.

In fact Andrew's leg was so bad that he was about to lose it. Luckily he came under the treatment of a professor who said that he could do some new work with him. I also called back in the original doctor who had taught Andrew and asked if there was anything else we could do, particularly with a view to controlling his pain.

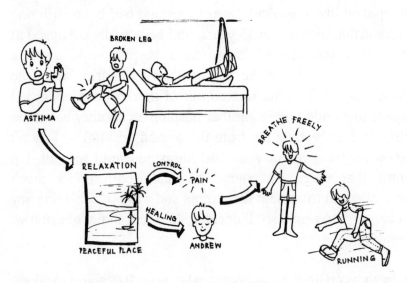

You see, Andrew was back on cortisone to control his pain, and cortisone and re-growth of bone are incompatible — so this was a real concern. The doctor who had helped Andrew with his asthma now taught Andrew to handle pain (so that Andrew no longer required cortisone), and to use his own mind, to enhance healing and to regrowing his leg bone.

So this was my introduction. All of this was quite remarkable to me and I was very, very impressed; so much so that I then got Andrew to teach me what it was all about.

Now for a little bit about my own personal background. I am what you call a left-brained person. I am an engineer and an army officer — it's hard to find someone who is a more "prove-it-to-me" type than that! I am the analytical type — I need everything to be seen in black and white, write it down, work it out, that sort of thing. I'm a left-brain dominant, analytical person. All of this "mind work" was not being proven to me personally. I could see what it was doing with my son Andrew, but I thought "It wouldn't work with me, not that sort of stuff".

In any case, I did what Andrew taught me, three times a day, 20 minutes a day — I'm a very persistent type of person. To get professional assistance I went to a consultant and he said to me "Sure you're doing it right — what you're doing is perfect". I said "Well I don't know for sure that I'm doing anything, so how can I prove it to myself?" He told me that two of the most difficult things to do are to lose weight and to give up smoking.

Well I didn't smoke but boy did I need to lose some weight! So he gave me a weight loss program and for six weeks I followed it three times a day, playing myself a tape — but nothing happened — absolutely nothing! (... or so I thought!). However, in the seventh week I lost 2 pounds; and then I lost 2 pounds in the eighth week, and then 2 pounds in the ninth

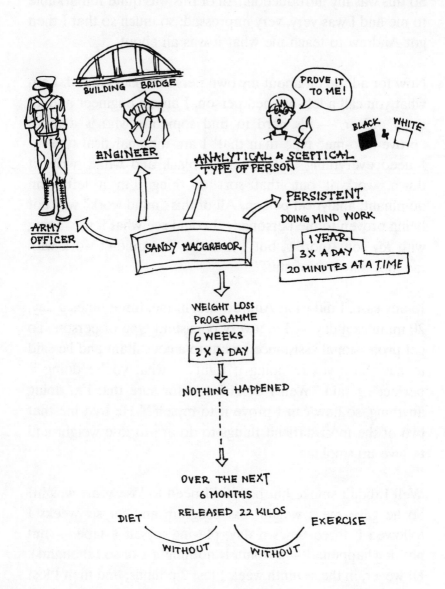

week. Do you know, over the next six months I lost 49 pounds! Yes, 49 pounds! (that's about 22 kilos). I did not do any exercise, nor did I go on a diet, until I had lost the weight. Had I done so, it would have meant that I was doing something else, other than using my mind, and I wanted the "mind" method to be proved to me. So that's precisely what I did. I worked at it, proved the method to myself, then I used the relaxation system to do many different things. One example is, whilst standing in front of a doctor, I could bring my pulse rate down to such a low rate that it was almost imperceptible, and could also reduce my blood pressure by about twenty points.

WOW!!

In January 1987 tragedy struck when my three teenage daughters were shotgun murdered by a crazed young young man. Going through grief takes quite a while and there is no short cut. However, by using the same system that Andrew had taught me to take control over myself, I was able to change feelings of hurt, anger, and revenge to feelings of love, acceptance and forgiveness. I developed an inner peace, just by using the same sort of system that I had used to release weight and relax.

My fortunes then changed a little in that I went to the United States to attend a six week course with Insight Awareness Seminars, which are quite fantastic! There are three Insight Seminars conducted in Australia and then the fourth one, in 1987, was conducted in the United States in California. An army colleague of mine had recommended that I check out Insight I in about 1982, and because of my very high regard for him I thought "Well if he thinks this is good and of real use then it must be OK" — so I did the first seminar.

Several years later, immediately after the death of my daughters this same friend's wife actually, "grabbed" me and virtually insisted that I do the next seminar — Insight II — to help me handle my grief. That was a great move. So from there I did Insight III and that's how I came to be at Insight IV in the United States.

At this seminar we had the leading people from around the world speaking to us on different topics. There was one speaker whose name was Steven Snyder, and he spoke for six to eight hours. Do you know he taught a room full of 60 people everything that I had taken 18 months to learn. It had taken me 18 months and he had taught a room full of people in six to eight hours! I thought "Great! His fast method is absolutely fantastic!" When I came home I gradually applied what I knew to my two younger children, Lara and Ian, who were six and four years old at the time.

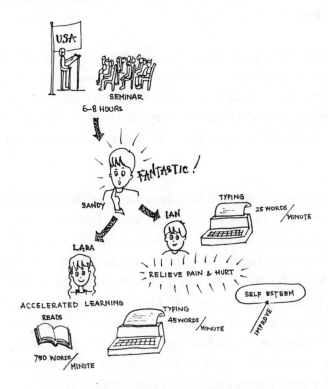

Lara went on to use accelerated reading and when she was 8 read at the rate of about 750 words per minute. Ian and Lara both learned to touch type on the computer with Lara then doing about 50 words per minute and Ian about 30 words a minute. Also they both use this same system to relieve pain and hurt; and to improve their own self-esteem.

I resolved to become more involved. I could see its value and I joined the Accelerated Learning Society. I could see how all the information I had learned is related to accelerated learning; not only study, memory and the like, but to life skills, applicable to most situations, for anybody, in any walk of life. One of the very first **keys** to accelerated learning is **relaxation**.

Then Steven Snyder came to Australia and I worked with him for 22 seminars — including work with the corporate sector, the general public, and children. Whilst I was working with Steven, I really perfected my knowledge of exactly what the method and system were all about. This is what I now teach.

You now have a picture of how I became involved and you can also learn this system. It's easy — just make sure you incorporate the techniques explained in this book. To help you, you could choose to listen to my audio tape *A Peaceful Place No. 2 (Guided Imagery)*, or you could make your own tape. All of you, everyone without exception, can actually relax and release stress within 20 to 30 seconds. There are many additional benefits that lead on from mastering relaxation and these you can achieve as well. More of that later, for now just remember "doing it does it".

Comfort Zones

Usually we all operate from within our Comfort Zone — a self imposed boundary outside of which we feel uncomfortable. Let's say that the circle in the diagram shown is the boundary of "where we feel comfortable". Outside uncomfortable, inside comfortable. An example may be public speaking. The image of ourselves could be as a poor public speaker and therefore our comfort zone is inside the circle. Outside the circle represents public speaking, an area of challenge which is new to us. The boundary of the circle is the wall of fear or block or doubt about our own abilities.

When we challenge this boundary and go through the "fear" into the unknown, we are in the area of new learning — an area where we make mistakes and an area of tension and anxiety.

Is it OK to make mistakes? Sure it is, that's how we learn. Other situations could involve a new job, meeting new people, or driving your car in a new suburb. Once you've gone outside your Comfort Zone a few times you feel more comfortable and so you have extended your comfort zone.

I am going to be able to show you a wonderful non stressful way of increasing your Comfort Zone, extending your learning and feeling good about yourself. In fact that's my responsibility with this book: "To take you into new areas of learning".

Role of the Subconscious

Why is change challenging? It is challenging because the role of the subconscious mind is to keep you where you are now — hence all your personality, habits, self image and memory will drive you when you "float" along, ie. no change will take place until you have consciously directed your subconscious mind to form a new habit.

The conscious mind directs the subconscious mind; it does that best when you are totally relaxed (in Alpha) thinking of one thing at a time. Remember the Comfort Zone expands when you consciously dare to risk — you may make mistakes and yet you will learn more. Using your subconscious mind to achieve means stress-free learning.

Exercise

What I would like you, the reader, to do now, is to take a pencil and write down, in the space provided below, five good things about yourself. Write them down and repeat them to yourself. Enough space has been left for you to come back and read the book again in a month, six months or whatever and add to the list. Note where you were at then and where you are at now.

....
....
....
....
....
....

....
....
....
....
....
....

Ongoing Support

I have a system of support in place which includes:

✦   Books and tapes (listed in the back of this book)

✦   Talks/Discussion/Follow up Meetings

✦   Seminars for children and adults in the public, educational and corporate areas, conducted by myself and my accredited trainers

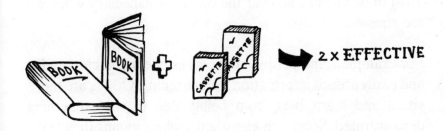

✦   Regular Newsletters to all people who require them (there is a small charge)

✦ I am always available to answer questions and I encourage you to write to me at PO Box 482, Lindfield NSW 2070 (Sydney, Australia) or call me on 61-2- 439 7188.

Many of the books and tapes available are also very useful for companies. In fact companies using accelerated learning methods train twice as many people more effectively, with the same budget.

To obtain maximum benefit from this book I urge you to follow all the exercises throughout the book.

Doing it doesn't...

Representational Styles

We all learn with all our senses, but often one of our senses dominates. From the science of Neurolinguistic Programming (NLP) we find that we learn and communicate with all our senses — sight, hearing, smell, taste, touch. These representational styles are: visual, auditory and kinesthetic. Most of us favour one over the others — especially when we are stressed.

For example some people are good listeners and can readily and easily absorb information from listening. Others are more visual and learn best from being able to see something demonstrated. Some are kinesthetic, which means they learn best from actually doing, or experiencing, in much the same way as you are doing now, by reading this book and doing the exercises yourself. If you love to learn by getting involved, then perhaps you would find greater benefit in actually attending discussion groups or seminars. I am a particularly good auditory person — I quite readily absorb information through my ears. However, when I was at university, I didn't learn from listening. The lecturer was busy writing on the blackboard as well as talking. I concentrated on copying down the notes (and daydreaming as well). I'd look at those notes a day or a week later but I didn't recognise the material! It was not until I actually went over the notes again and "experienced" them that I started to absorb the information.

Most people are dominated by one or two of the three primary representational styles, being: auditory, visual or kinesthetic. → *Also our Expectation about the task..*

A rough average of how people learn is:

—   50-60% of learning takes place via the most dominant representational style

—   30-40% the next most dominant

—   10-20% the least dominant

It can be quite frustrating in a marriage situation when one partner is visually dominant and one is auditory dominant. This is the case in my family. My wife is visual and sometimes has selective hearing when I'm talking. This is not a criticism — I can certainly be the same — it's quite natural. Often I will explain something and think that Sandra is listening and that she has got it. Later Sandra may claim not to know about it. It might be a lesson to me about my communication skills, or timing, but it certainly can create misunderstanding and communication breakdown. It can be quite frustrating, there's no doubt about it (we now have an agreement that if I want Sandra to take some action on what it is that I have said then I must write it down, or she repeats it back to me. It seems to work!).

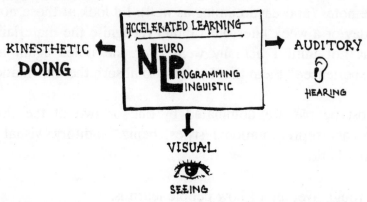

My younger son is very kinesthetic. He used to have stories read to him, which he loved. But what he would do when the story was being read was play. He'd play with his cars, with his planes, whatever it might be, and he'd run around the room — but make no mistake — he knew every word that was being said at any time. He knew exactly where the story was up to. He was probably processing kinesthetically, and being auditory as well — he needed to be able to do something whilst listening. Now it can be frustrating reading to a kid when you think he is not paying attention. "Pay attention, listen to the story! You wanted me to read to you, do you want to hear it or not?!" ... but he heard every word!

Many school teachers come across kinesthetic kids and in some instances they are labelled hyperactive. I have even heard of situations whereby children have been given drugs to calm them down! There are other ways of teaching these children. It is very important if you are a teacher to know whether your students are visual, auditory or kinesthetic. When teaching any group of people these three representational systems always need to be covered.

Exercise

Here's another exercise. Take a pencil, and once again in the space provided, write down why you decided to read this book. What is your expectation, what do you want out of this book? You could even ask your friends to have a glance at the book and see what they would get out of it. What I'm promoting here is to have a discussion with yourself, and others, to work out what reasons you have to read, study and do the exercises in this book. Whilst this may be difficult for you to do, I encourage you to share your reasons with someone. There's always quite a variety of reasons from all those involved.

....
....
....
....
....
....
....

Let me now share with you what I'm going to cover — what my reason or aim is, for writing this book.

✦ Firstly I am going to show you how you can obtain relaxation and release stress quickly. To achieve this though there is one proviso, and that is — that you want to do it! If you do not really want to do it, then that probably means that you are not ready for it yet. I guess it's a bit like giving up smoking, if you don't really want to do it then you will not succeed in giving it up. The same with relaxation and releasing stress, there will be a "struggle" going on in your mind and you cannot possibly achieve relaxation unless you want to do it.

✦ Secondly I will cover accelerated learning skills. In fact what will happen with accelerated learning skills is that you can experience some of the skills by reading and doing the exercises in this book — we've already started. The "how to apply it" to things like study and work will also emerge. Of course the actual study you will need to do yourself!

✦ Thirdly, I will show you a way to achieve your goals faster. The goal can be whatever you like, for instance wanting to relieve pain, wanting more self-confidence, wanting to give up smoking or to release weight (we don't say lose weight any more because if you lose something you want to go and find it again), achieving success, increasing sales, controlling anger, overcoming insomnia, better communication, achieving a certain mark in an exam. Whatever your goal may be, you will find a way of achieving that goal faster — much faster than it took me when I first learned about how to do this, and we'll come to the reasons why.

Is the reason why you decided to read this book covered by the three points above? Look back to what you wrote down in the last exercise.

Questions and Answers

Will I be able to achieve all three?

Yes, you will. You will be able to achieve relaxation in 30 seconds. You will obtain a way to clarify and achieve a goal faster. Say if your goal is to obtain high distinctions in final exams or to release weight, then you'll be able to start working on it in this book. It could be your primary aim for reading this book and you will certainly be able to experience and obtain some accelerated learning skills.

How important is having a goal?

One of the things that the science of dreams has shown is that happiness is a journey. Happiness comes from moving towards a goal, not actually getting it.

To remain happy always have a goal that you are working towards. A famous guru describes the secret of happiness as "BE HAPPY". In other words a verb — a doing word.

What about recall and memory can these be improved?

Yes, absolutely — that will be covered, in fact there will be some exercises on that. I will tell you about memory and how it occurs and how you'll be able to put information into the brain whereby you'll be able to recall more easily. Our memory is fantastic — it's recall that we need. To improve recall we need to take the correct action to ensure that the information goes to long term memory.

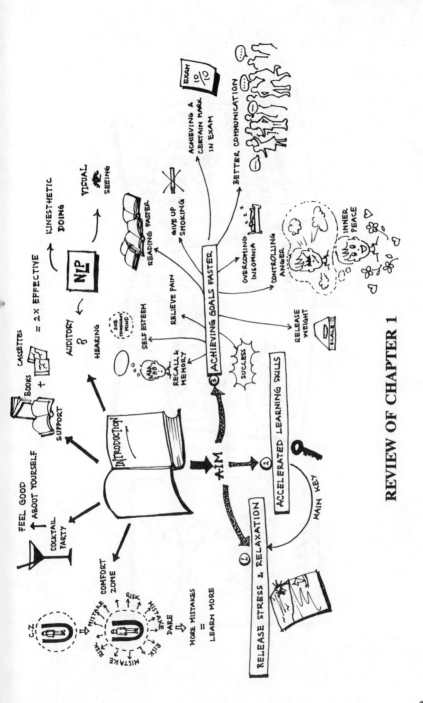

REVIEW OF CHAPTER 1

PREVIEW OF CHAPTER 2

2

THE BRAIN

I am going to tell you about the way this works for me; in other words I'm going to go through my left brain, analytical approach. It's the best approach for sceptics, of which I am one of the biggest! I'll start by telling you about the brain and how it works: how memory works, how recall works. I want to demonstrate to you that this is scientific. In the last 30 years a lot of work has been done on the brain and scientists have proven many new facts. Prior to that, people who used the brain differently were either labelled "loonies" or "brilliant". There are new breakthroughs happening all the time and some of the recent ones I will be passing on to you. It's a good idea to keep abreast of all new developments, because there are probably many new things still to come that will revolutionise learning yet again.

I found the following quotation from the 1962 edition of the Reader's Digest: "OUR HUMAN BODY Its Wonders & Its Care" (page 113) quite interesting:

The unconscious mind is a marvellous storehouse. The most wonderful part of your mind is undoubtedly the unconscious, which lies below the recoverable memory and is thousands of times larger. We don't yet know very much about the unconscious mind, but we are learning fast and some day may know how to tap its great powers. Your unconscious mind contains many millions of past experiences that, so far as your conscious mind knows, are lost forever. By means of several devices we now know how to bring back lost memories. One method is "free association", used by psychiatrists. If a patient lets his conscious mind wander at will, it can give him clues to forgotten things which, skilfully pursued by the doctor, will bring up whole networks of lost ideas and forgotten terrors. There are certain drugs which also help in this process; hypnotism, too, can be of tremendous value in exploring a patient's unconscious. Many psychologists believe that we can make more use of our unconscious minds. Innumerable people have found that they can profitably "talk to" their unconscious. Some people find that they can bid themselves to wake up at a certain time in the morning. You can sometimes even improve your tomorrow's mood if you will say to yourself when you go to bed — and believe it — that you will be more cheerful in the morning.

Haven't we come a long way in 30 years!

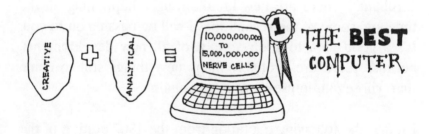

The brain itself has got 10 to 15 billion nerve cells and each nerve cell has got thousands of contact points. The human brain of course is the best computer that we know of, and it's 50,000 years old — it has not changed, in man, for at least 50,000 years. Another very important point: the brain is the only organ in the body that continues to make new connections, as long as it is activated, as long as it is used.

It is the only organ in the body that continues to develop, isn't that nice to know? The major thing is, we need to use it, and keep on using it right up until death. Just a brief word on senility: if you believe that old people go senile — guess what could happen to you when you get older? Your belief system is very important and brings about what happens in your life.

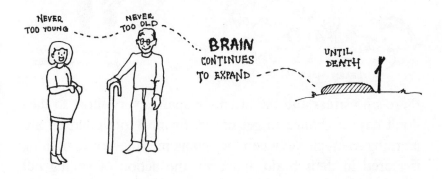

Now if you really believe that when people get old they go senile, then you may go senile. You may not, but belief systems can really help to create reality! So that is one belief that should definitely be discarded, unless of course there is some other factor to be considered, such as a medical condition. How many of you have heard of people who are over 90 or even 100 whose mind is still quite active — they're reading, discussing, playing cards — lots of things? Their physical body may let them down but their mind is active, and it can be, and it is. As long as you keep using your brain it will develop. So a fantastic start as far as senility is concerned would be to change your belief system, about old people going senile.

Children

Did you know that from 0 to 5 years old a child learns more
facts than it takes to get a university degree? A degree such
as law, medicine or engineering for example — and they have
fun doing it! In fact children love learning! It's enjoyable, as

there's no stress and the attention span is very short so they
don't have a chance to get bored. From 0 to 5 children are
learning so much, yet when they come into the world, nothing
is stored in their brain, not even the action of yelling out
"Mummy I want food". They do learn to get that message
across pretty soon though. Babies do not have the knowledge
(or the physical ability and awareness) to roll over, or play
with their fingers, or talk — no communication skills, nothing
at all, except this yell of course as soon as they're born. They
learn at a fantastic rate.

One of the reasons they learn is because absolutely
everything is new and they are so eager to learn that their
mind is like an "information absorbing" sponge. In fact a lot
of research is now being done to prove that genius is not only
born, but also made; research is also being done about
children learning in the womb. Genius really can be created,

it *has* happened, and there are several case histories.

Genius

Talking about genius for a moment, what percentage of our brain do we use? Do you have any idea? Only four to five per cent of our brain is what we use! Genius uses five to six per cent, which is really only just a fraction more? Now that doesn't mean to say that we **can** use 100%, because we don't know, (scientists haven't told us what the other 94% of our brain is used for). But what we can do by using our brains better is increase the total capacity of our brain. If we can

use both the left and right sides of the brain and the conscious and the subconscious mind, we are then going to be able to increase our brain capacity by possibly 10% (who knows — pick a figure yourself). So if you go from using 4% of your brain to 4.4% then you're getting well up towards 5% which is towards genius isn't it? You **can** do that. That's what accelerated learning is about — ways in which we can learn more, retain it, recall it, and have fun doing it!

Brain: Left (Analytical) and Right (Creative)

What are some of the features of left brain people? For instance I said I was analytical, prove-it-to-me, work-it-out, that sort of thing — I'm a left brain person. What are some of the other things in the left brain? Maths, numbers, logic, sequence, linearity, judgement, speech — language, (the English language at least because the Japanese language, for example, which uses symbols and "drawings", is learned in the right side of the brain). The words and timing of a song are in the left brain, but the musical aspect — the tune of a song — is in the right brain. Spatial skills and manipulation fall in the right brain. Painting, art, colour, music, imagination, creativity, daydreaming — that beautiful state that we often get rapped over the knuckles for — it's a great state (you're allowed to daydream in accelerated learning) that's a way to learn — are all right brain activities.

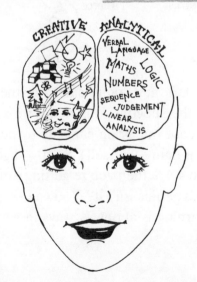

So now we have a list of probable left and right brain functions — probable. There is always someone who breaks the rule, so there is nothing 100% about this. Therefore from now on I will refer to the two sides of the brain as the "analytical side" and the "creative side".

Research varies — some shows that the Analytical Side is on the right side of the brain for over 17% of people (most left handers would fall into this category). Many people who suffer from dyslexia have their dominant brain on the same side as the dominant hand (with which they write). How do we know about the two sides of the brain? There is a machine called the electro-encephalograph which scientists use to measure the impulses that are in the brain. In fact, the left brain and the right brain have actually been cut in half. This has occurred when someone has had a tumour for instance, or severe and constant epileptic fits which cannot be controlled by the usual drugs.

Generally speaking the left and right brain constantly communicate with each other, but when the brain is cut in half the two halves can not communicate with each other; also, once cut, the two sides can never grow back together again. In this way, scientists have actually been able to measure what a person does with the left brain and with the right brain. These different activities can physically be measured on the electro-encephalograph.

Most of you have probably seen the electro-encephalograph on television — it's that machine on the back of the hospital bed in the doctors' series — the one that looks like a TV set. There are wavy lines going up and down and across the screen. When there is no energy in the mind and when you're dead the wavy line is gone. The wave becomes a straight line across the screen — waaaahhhhhhhhhhhhhh! You're dead. We've got a machine (the electro-encephalograph) to tell us when we're dead — science tells us! Your heart can still be beating, your blood can still be flowing, everything in your body can still moving, but when you're brain dead — you're dead. That's when the life support equipment can be unplugged, everything turned off, because you're brain dead, and without the life support equipment your heart stops beating, and your blood stops flowing. So we have a machine to tell us when we're dead. The difference between dead and alive is the energy measured by the machine. When you're dead that energy has gone; it's gone somewhere but we don't know where. Science hasn't told us where it's gone; we can speculate, but that is not part of what I am getting into in this book. (I welcome talking about it and do so in the book *Switch On to Your Inner Strength*).

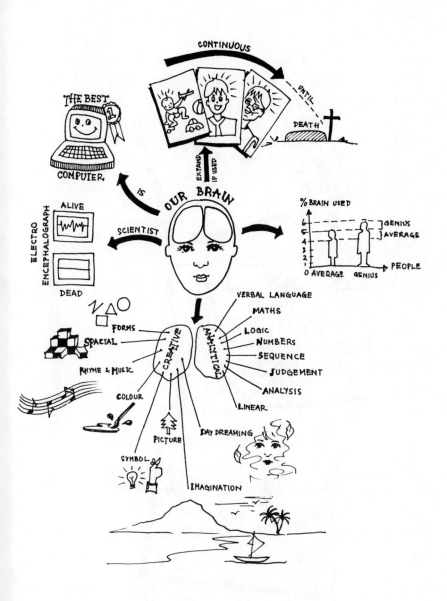

REVIEW OF CHAPTER 2

PREVIEW OF CHAPTER 3

3

THE 88% POWER — YOUR SUBCONSCIOUS MIND

Your Subconscious Mind

The circle in the diagram on the next page represents the mind. The shaded area shows the 12% which is the conscious mind — the remaining 88% is the subconscious mind. Between the conscious and the subconscious mind there is a "filter" (dotted line) which is the Reticular Activating System.

This filter is very useful, in fact it keeps us sane by protecting our minds from superfluous, unnecessary information. We can certainly use it to our advantage. We do use it naturally, but we can use it more, and you'll learn exactly what its function is and how you can use it.

In the subconscious mind resides our memory, all our habits, all our personality, and our self-image; it's all there — what a great storehouse. Even what we subconsciously think of ourselves is in there. The subconscious mind is very, very powerful.

Some people say we have a mind that has a conscious part

and a subconscious part. That's OK too. It's just semantics. I choose to call it conscious mind and subconscious mind.

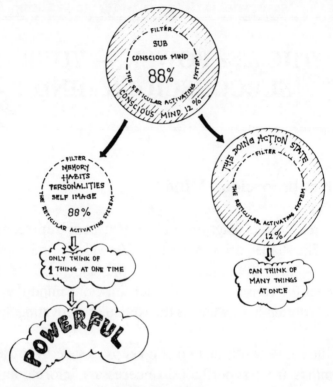

Programming the Subconscious

When I was eight years old classrooms consisted of desks and chairs that were bolted to the floor. The teacher generally spoke from a desk at the front of the room near a huge blackboard. One day I was called on to draw an elephant on the blackboard (it must have been nature study or perhaps geography). I heard quite a bit of muffled laughter behind me and I don't blame them now for laughing, because it was probably the funniest elephant anyone had ever seen. I was really embarrassed when the teacher smiled. "Even the teacher laughing at me as well" I thought. Thank goodness it was break time, but the kids in the playground didn't let up. "You can't draw, you can't draw" with an accusing finger

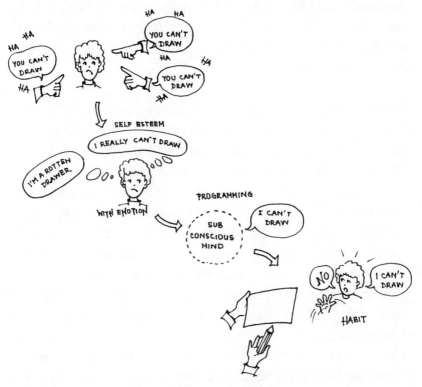

levelled at me. At that time I told myself "I can't draw", and "I hate drawing" and "I'll never draw again!".

Does it sound at all familiar? Have you ever had a humiliating, embarrassing situation like that? It's a classic case of self esteem being damaged (by my classmates and the teacher laughing at my drawing) followed by my damaging self talk (I can't draw — I hate drawing — I'll never draw again). All this, done in an atmosphere of great embarrassment and emotion so that my self image (I can't draw) was indelibly imprinted on my subconscious mind. So strong was this, and done with such emotion that when I was 15 years old doing a social studies project, my subconscious mind overruled my conscious mind by saying "What are you trying to do? – you know you can't draw! Put that pen down!" I remember it vividly even to the extent of going to find a picture of a seal that I could trace.

True for some of you I am sure – that some time in the past you had something similar happen, whereby your self esteem was punctured and this was reinforced by your own self talk. It's the way things can happen, but the good news is that you can reprogram something like that. Remember, self image is caused by self esteem, and self esteem commences with self-talk, firstly by telling yourself (for example) "Hey I can't draw". Self talk either boosts or lowers your self esteem. It's how you think about yourself that goes into your subconscious mind and then bounces it back to you: "Hey you can't draw". That then becomes your self-image. Your subconscious mind takes over from that moment onwards and it lets you know that you can't draw. Every time you take up a pen that's exactly what comes from your subconscious mind up into your conscious mind. However, as I said before, that can be reprogrammed by using Alpha techniques. Alpha is the scientific name given to the level of energy in your brain when you are in a state of light relaxation.

The conscious mind is the "doing", "action state", where we spend most of the time. Those of you who have never before done conscious relaxation and "gone into Alpha" when reading are probably now in the Beta state – the state where you are only using your conscious mind. It is a state in which we can think of many things and do many things at once. However, to work with the subconscious mind you think of only one thing at a time — this is the Alpha state.

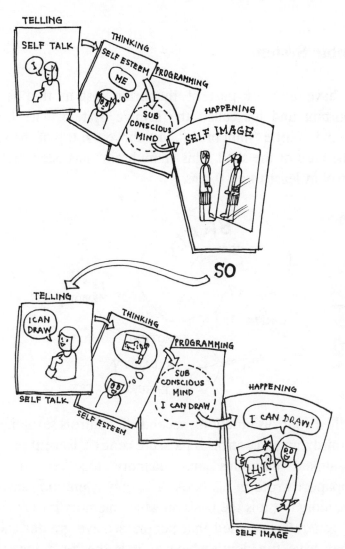

Real learning takes place when the conscious mind directs the subconscious mind to receive information and store it in a part of the brain from which it can be easily recalled. We will learn how to activate the subconscious mind and have it directed by the conscious mind.

Limbic System

We have another part of the brain system that is very important and it's called the Limbic System. The Limbic System is a little "mini brain", just above the top of the spine, at the base of the skull. This "mini brain" has been found to control at least three things.

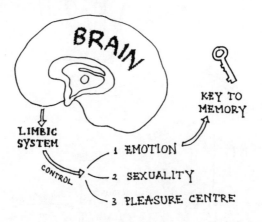

Firstly it controls emotions, secondly it controls sexuality and the third thing it controls is pleasure centres. Recent research has linked emotions and memory together. In 1971 Rappaport wrote in his book "not only is emotion involved in memory but it is the basis on which memory is organised". It is generally accepted that people achieve greater success if they have fun doing whatever it is they're doing (that's using positive emotion). Today the whole of the accelerated learning movement uses emotion as a key aspect for accelerated learning. This aspect of how emotion can really have an effect will be emphasised and worked with in this book. Remember my personal experience of releasing weight? (remember, not "lose weight" otherwise we will only go and "find" it again) — it took me seven weeks before I released 2 pounds. This was because I didn't use emotion — I didn't know of its importance at that time. Now people who use these techniques are releasing 2 pounds in the second week, when they have that as their specific goal or aim.

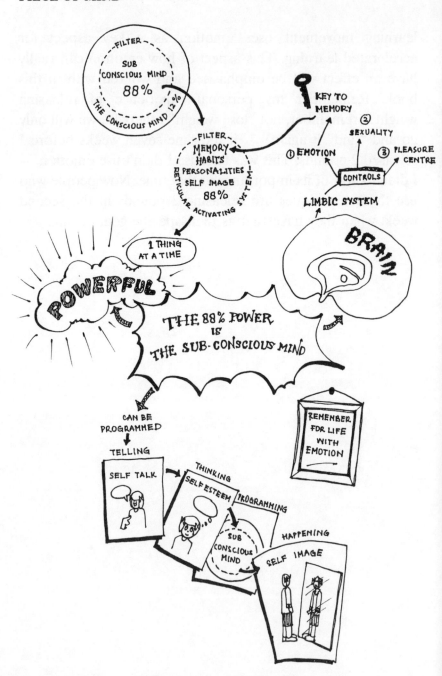

REVIEW OF CHAPTER 3

The job of the subconscious mind is to keep you where you are now — with all the habits that you've got now — whether they support you or not.

The job of the conscious mind is to put into the subconscious what you want.

PREVIEW OF CHAPTER 4

4

MIND CHARTING

Introduction to Mind Charting

What I would like to do at this stage is stop talking about the mind and the brain and now turn to a "doing" activity called **Mind Charting**. (I have heard and read this described as "Mind Mapping", "Mindscapes" and "Mind Clustering" — I'll call it **"Mind Charting"**). It is an important topic for academic accelerated learning and its uses can also be applied to achieving life skills goals faster. Many people are able to complete mind charts in the relaxed focused concentration state, whilst others may do them in the active Beta state. I have found the activity of doing them, in whatever state, important. By now you probably realise that because it is so important you will find Mind Charts throughout the book (done by Monika Kobus).

Accelerated learning strives to involve the whole brain. One great technique is to present information in two ways. Written work (words) involves the analytical side of the brain whilst Mind Charting uses pictures and colours which involve the creative side of the brain. In this book a summary is presented in two different Mind Chart formats. These Mind

Charts appear at the front and at the end of each chapter (they summarise the book).

The idea is to switch the mind onto the information about to be presented (first Mind Chart) and then after the information has been presented, to quickly revise it with the second Mind Chart. All the Mind Charts need colour. I urge you to colour in as many as possible, especially those that have been specifically prepared for colouring in, ie. Pages 130, 161, and 191. Mind Charting is an accelerated learning tool, or skill if you like. The subconscious mind itself does not think chronologically. The conscious mind thinks in an analytical way — we have trained it to think like that. Most of us commence analytical/logical learning at school.

All sorts of thoughts come from all over the place. Right now how many different things are you thinking about? Probably not just what you are reading about — other thoughts and

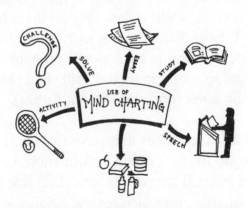

distractions are always creeping in around the edges of our mind. When you think about a problem, or an essay you have to write, or a challenge facing you, look at all the things that come into your mind at once. No chronological order, many thoughts, ideas, and patterns come randomly into your mind. You then sort it out and record it in a chronological way. One use of Mind Charting is that it helps you to record these thoughts in a non chronological way. Mind Charting is a mechanism for note taking, for thinking. It is a mechanism for problem solving and for remembering and doing something as we think of it, as the thought enters our mind.

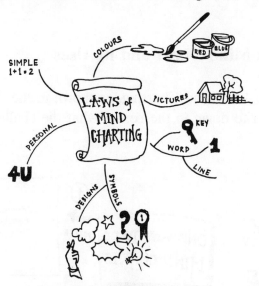

The Laws of Mind Charting

The laws of Mind Charting are very simple. As the thought enters your mind you jot it down, not in note form, but in a simple diagram or symbol, using colour, if that's the way the thought comes in.

Use pictures, lots of little pictures — a little house, little tree in front of it for example. Branch along to the next picture (thought), or use one key word per line; use symbols. When we take notes we all use symbols already, so use them for Mind Charting, use designs — any designs which are special for you. Now what that means is that every time you do a Mind Chart, that Mind Chart is for you and only you. It is not for somebody else. Isn't that a great thing, the fact that you're able to record all the information that you want to know in the way you want to know it?

Making a Mind Chart and its Uses

✦ Step 1 to Mind Charting, as shown in the diagram, is to write down in the centre what the challenge is.

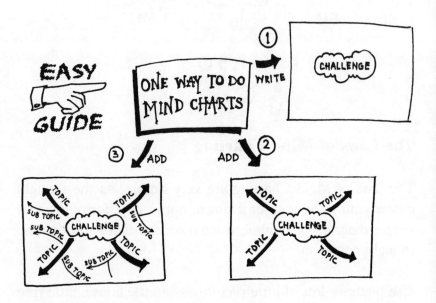

✦ Step 2 is to have branches for topics, as they come into your mind.

✦ Step 3 is to have sub branches for those topics, everything that affects that sub branch.

So while you're thinking of a challenge, say of writing a music essay, suddenly something comes into your mind such as the different types of music, like classical, baroque, jazz, rock, or perhaps great composers like Mozart, Chopin, Wagner, or instruments in an orchestra. These are all aspects that would go in different parts of a Mind Chart.

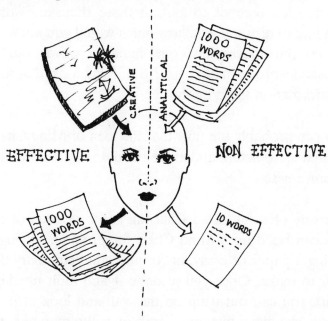

You can use this sort of Mind Chart when taking notes as you listen to somebody. That is one way, but if that's disturbing to you then of course don't do it, just take your notes in the normal way. The idea of Mind Charting is to build up a picture. How powerful is a picture? A picture is worth — how many words? — a thousand words. We've all heard that saying so often. You look at a picture for ten seconds and straight away you can describe it, probably using a thousand words. The information from the picture has gone straight through to the creative brain. The creative side of the brain thinks in pictures.

So the information from the picture goes straight into the creative side of the brain and then you can describe it with the other side of the brain — the analytical side of the brain. On the other hand though, if you had a thousand words and you had ten seconds to look at those thousand words and then had to reproduce it, how much would you know? You'd be flat out to produce one hundred words out of the thousand words wouldn't you? But if you looked at a picture — information flows easily.

You can probably see now that the idea of Mind Charting is to build up a picture and as we build up a picture that is how we can revise.

One way of using Mind Charting is for revision of a topic. You can build up a Mind Chart for problem solving or for writing a paper or essay, or for any other summary that you want to make. Once you've done it and built up this Mind Chart, you can put it up on the wall and look at it — very quickly just like a picture — and you will remember, with the creative side of your brain. The next day make really sure you look at it again, if your walls at home or in the office are getting full, then take the Mind Chart down, and put it in a scrap book, or your note book. Look at it a week later, then

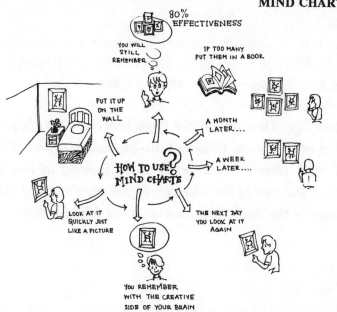

a month later, and each time revise only what you don't know. Experimentation has shown that a year later there is a 90% success rate in remembering the information, through the use of Mind Charts. Pretty powerful!

Take a moment now to look at the Mind Charts on pages 130, 157, and 204. These are three different kinds of Mind Charts — choose one of these styles or make your own.

Exercise

Take some coloured pencils, and spend about five minutes making a Mind Chart of the information you have read so far.

A Mind Chart of this book (so far) has been prepared by Monika Kobus (isn't she good at it?). What you can do is colour it in — perhaps compare it to your own, remembering that anything you prepare yourself is much more powerful. Turn to the next two pages to see Monika's Mind Chart.

A Good Tip: Throughout the book preview each chapter by looking at the Mind Chart at the beginning of the chapter. Read each chapter then revise it by looking at the Mind Chart at the end of the chapter. If you ever want to quickly summarise the book, just look at these Mind Charts.

USE COLOUR !

Research into using colour in the last ten years has shown:

- ✦ Memory is improved by up to 82%

- ✦ A 70% time saving is made in reading

- ✦ Reading motivation increases by up to 80%

- ✦ Understanding is 73% easier

USE COLOUR FOR –

Notes, lectures, study, mind charting and everywhere you can.

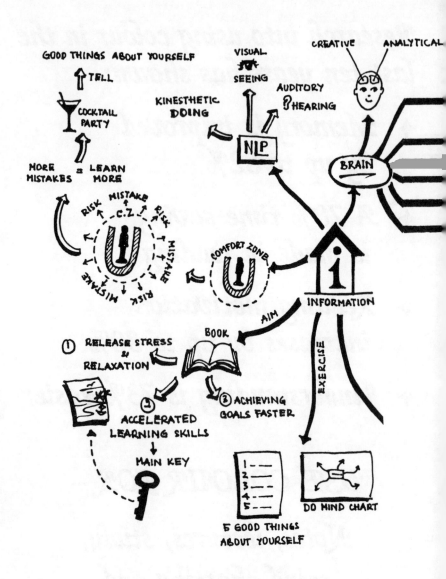

REVIEW OF CHAPTERS 1 — 4

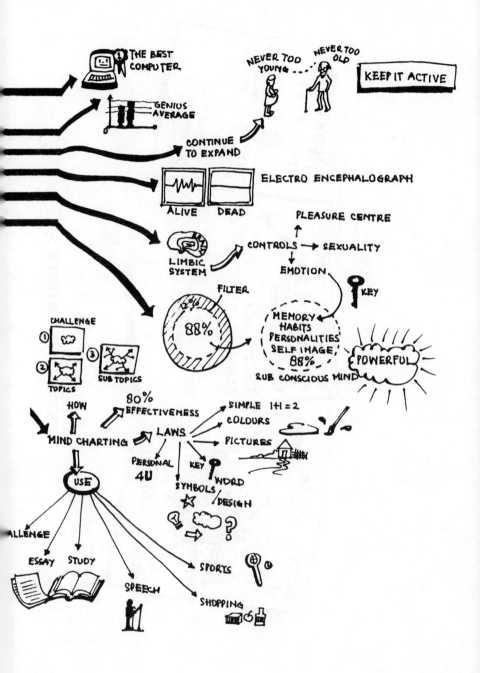

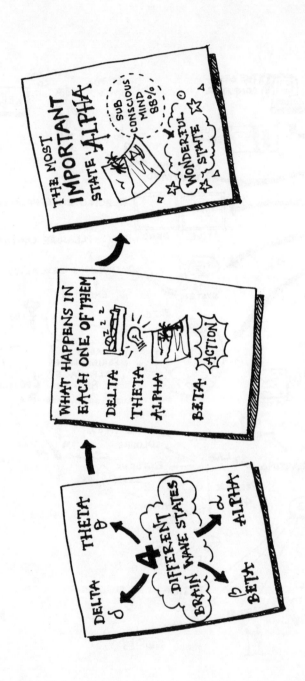

PREVIEW OF CHAPTER 5

5

BRAIN WAVE STATES

Scientists have measured the different brain wave states and named them Delta, Theta, Alpha and Beta. Some of you may be thinking: what's all this business about brain wave states: Delta, Theta, Alpha, Beta? – it's na-na-nou-nou stuff (blame the scientists for the names). Well, it's not na-na-nou-nou, it's scientific. Brain waves are measured by the machine mentioned before, the electro-encephalograph. The electro-encephalograph actually measures how many cycles there are going across that screen in one second; the cycles vary in speed – cycles per second, and however many cycles per second there are, determines the brain wave state. So it's a measurement of brain activity.

Delta State

The Delta state is the sleep state, the deep dreamless sleep state – 0.5 cycles per second, (it can't start off at zero because zero means dead), so 0.5 cycles per second up to about 3.5 cycles per second is the Delta Brain Wave State – the brain wave pattern when we are asleep. Coma is in fact at about 0.5 cycles per second, so a person who is in a coma has a complete cycle every two seconds. Deep dreamless sleep is the state of healing and regeneration. When you're sick you sleep more because the body heals itself naturally during this state.

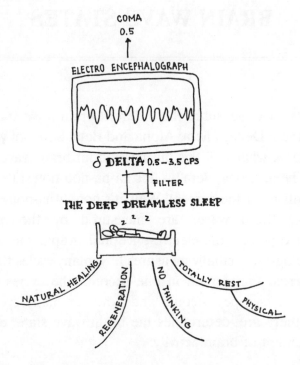

As adults we need about eight hours rest a day. Now eight hours rest a day does not necessarily mean eight hours sleep a day. We can actually function with four hours sleep a day, but the other four hours should be in a restful state. It can be in the Alpha state or it can be in the Theta state, but it must be resting, we need eight hours rest a day.

If you are not an adult, in other words you're still growing taller, then you need more than eight hours rest a day. Eight hours rest could mean six hours sleep and two hours rest.

Now if you're used to having eight hours sleep, then please don't endeavour to go straight to four hours sleep because you will tire out. What you need to do is to go to 7½ hours sleep, then to 7 hours sleep, then to 6½ then to 6 and each half hour you come down, you do two things. One is, you take a month in which to do it. The second thing is that you actually have the rest period in the Alpha state or the Theta state.

Theta State

The Theta state is 3½ to 7 cycles per second. The Theta state is the creativity state, an inspiration state. This is where real creativity can come through. It is also a state of very high suggestibility and a body healing state. This is the state we

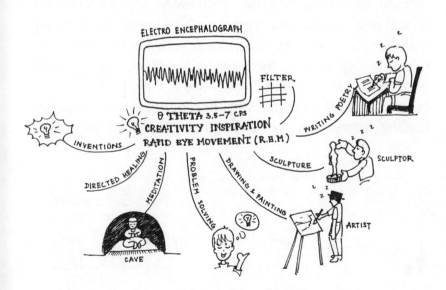

are in when we have dreams. Rapid eye movement, or REM as it is commonly known, happens when the eyes are closed. It is just a little flickering which indicates that you're having a dream — in the Theta state. Many great creators, artists, musicians, inventors, etc, actually work in the Theta state and come up with brilliant creations or inventions. (They can also work in the Alpha state, and that's what we will be doing). Louise Hay and Petrea King healed themselves using the Theta state. Dr Ainslie Meares taught his patients to work at the Theta level. He helped many people with all sorts of healing, and he wrote several books. He also taught Ian Gawler who had bone cancer and lost his leg. He was diagnosed as terminally ill, and the cancer was spreading. He used the Theta state, this high suggestibility state, this body healing state, to heal himself. We have all heard of people who have been diagnosed with cancer, and then have had what is called a "spontaneous remission". Most of the medical profession describe a recovery with no apparent reason as a "spontaneous remission", which means that they really don't know why the person recovered; there is no scientific explanation for their cure. However, generally speaking, what has been happening is that the person has been "working" on themselves, healing themselves, and this healing happens in the Theta state. Scientists no longer

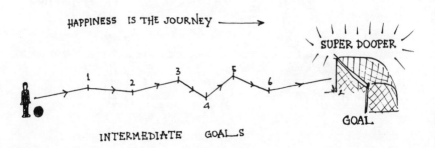

ignore spontaneous remission; there are now a number of research projects going on around the world and hopefully much more evidence will be established when science has proved this healing process.

Dreams are quite fantastic. There has been a lot of dream study done and I want to mention two things in particular that have emerged from dream study. One is that happiness comes from moving towards a goal, not actually getting it. It's not the destination, it is the journey that is important. Now of course there is some happiness in the achievement of a goal, however it is the journey which matters. Many organisations teach goal setting and what they all teach now is that just before you get to the goal, just when you're about to "make it", you set another goal! Remember, happiness is the journey towards the goal, not the destination. This is applied the world over to goals and goal setting, the fact that you need to set another goal, always moving onwards.

Another thing that has come out of dream study is that early morning dreams release stress. If you don't have these stress-releasing dreams, stress can build up in your body.

Who uses an alarm clock to wake up in the morning? I am sure there are many. An alarm clock can really startle you out of a deep sleep. Remember that the Theta state is the dream state and these early morning dreams are the body's inbuilt mechanism to release stress. If you interrupt your natural dream process, or go straight from deep sleep to wide awake, then stress builds up in your body. Experiments have been done with rats, (and also with people). What researchers did with rats was put them in a cage, and observe what happened when they were denied the dream process.

Rats also have rapid eye movement when they are in the dream state — just the same as you and I. So what happened in the experiment was that the scientists only allowed the rats to be either asleep or awake. Awake or asleep, that's all — no dreams. As soon as they started to have the REM they were in the dream state, so were woken up with a little pin prick. Do you know what happened to those rats? They got so angry, so disturbed, so anxious, that they started gnawing, then eating each other and they all died in a fairly short space of time. Now, if you use an alarm clock you are not releasing your stress, because the early morning dreams are the stress release dreams, of which you will deprive yourself.

So what can you do about it? How many of you have really looked forward to going on a journey, a great holiday, for which you know you have to get going very early the next morning. To start this journey, you need to wake up at 3.00

in the morning. You set the alarm clock, you place a request for an early morning wake-up call — just in case ... and guess what happens at one minute to three? — you wake up, don't you? You wake up and reach across to turn off the alarm before it even goes off: "Oh I'm awake and I didn't need the alarm clock." Guess what's happened? You've gone through those stress release dreams because you've woken up naturally, by yourself. There was a lot of emotion involved in looking forward to your holiday, so you were easily able to program your mind. **You can** program your mind so that you can wake up without an alarm clock — all you need is a little bit of passion or emotion when you're doing it, or a really good reason not to need an alarm clock. Well, I've now just given you a good one — let your body release stress naturally.

So what I'd suggest you start doing from now on is to set your alarm clock for 5.30 in the morning (or whatever is necessary for you) — make sure it's a music alarm clock, nice soft gentle music as the "alarm", but then you program yourself to wake up at 5.25 am. (I've got two tapes of baroque masters all at 56 to 64 beats per minute titled *Accelerated Learning Music* which would be appropriate to wake up to — see page 234. The heart beat gets in time with the music so that from deep sleep you just drift into Alpha or Theta state and then wake up — after your dreams). You can then just gently lean across and turn off the alarm clock, or stay there until 5.30 doing your Alpha exercises. The main thing is to wake up naturally, before the alarm goes off, so that you release the stress in your body. Eventually get rid of the alarm clock.

Here is a way that dreams and stress work. If you happen to see something particularly stressful, like a car accident for example, and at the scene there's blood and gore and it's pretty gruesome. As you go past it you see it all, and everything goes into your mind. Or you might see something horrific on the television, or hear bad news on the radio or notice newspaper headlines — it all goes into your mind and it can create a form of stress. It's not all your fault that you've noticed bad news, but it still goes into your mind. After having seen the car accident you might think: "Oh no, a car accident, what a mess", and a little bit of stress goes into your body. That night you might dream about the car accident. You have an early morning dream about a car accident — it's the natural way of relieving that stress because it's above the level that it ought to be. As soon as you have that dream about a car accident, (or something else traumatic) generally speaking you wake up and go "Whewww it was only a dream". Some of you however, say, "Oh no, I'm going to have a car accident", which of course creates more stress and that's when repetitive dreams can occur. With a repetitive dream it's as

though it's telling you: "Hey, you haven't got the message yet". All that fear about having a car accident, or whatever, is recycled, and your body will naturally relieve the stress by having the dream again, ... and again, ... and again ... until you get the message. A good way to handle a stress release dream is to tell yourself "It was only a dream and everything's fine". It's your conscious mind that lets you know that the whole "accident" is not real and that it was "only a dream". This has all come from the study of dreams.

By the way, do you know that you are not responsible for all your thoughts — sometimes you cannot help what comes into your mind. For instance, it wasn't your fault that you saw that car accident was it? It wasn't your fault that you noticed other horrific things, and you didn't cause the things that happened. Look at the crazy things that happen in dreams — are you responsible for them? No — not all of them. That's good to know, isn't it?

This Theta brain wave state, the state for high suggestibility and body healing, is also the state for meditation. Yogis and maharishis and similar sorts of people who go to the Tibetan mountains and meditate for up to 23 hours a day are in this state — many people who meditate are in this state. The aim is to still the mind. You're thinking is as "clear as a bell", and the brain wave cycles per second are extremely low — between 3½ to 7. You know when you're in this Theta state because what happens is that your mind is very clear, lucid, and yet you have no sense of your body. It is as though you don't feel your hands or legs. It's a great feeling. I practise this for up to two hours every morning — it's much better than sleep.

Exercise

Do the following exercise by quietly contemplating each question. Write down the answers if you wish and/or discuss it with someone close to you.

✦ *Think of a situation when you're stressed.*

✦ *How do you act — what do you do to show your stress?*

✦ *What would you like to do instead?*

Alpha State

The Alpha state is 7 to 13 cycles a second. This is the relaxation state. It is the state we're really interested in and the one with which we're going to work. The Alpha state is the most important state. It opens up access to that 88% power of the subconscious mind. You need to be in the Alpha state to get to the subconscious mind effectively. Alpha is the relax-

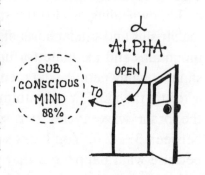

ation state, the state wherein stress vanishes. When you go into the Alpha brain wave state, your stress goes, you're relaxed, thereby allowing you into the subconscious mind. When you're there you can change your self image, you can change your personal habits, you can implant thoughts, set goals, study, read, etc. The Alpha state focuses concentration — you can only think of one thing at a time. The minute that you start thinking of two or three things at a time you've gone into the Beta state and you're out of Alpha. So if you're reading in the Alpha state, (and I'll explain how to do that) and you hear a train go past or a plane fly overhead or you hear someone knock on the front door, and it distracts you, then you're in the Beta state. You're in the Beta state when you're thinking of two things (or more) at a time. To go on reading you will learn to quickly go back to reading in the Alpha state.

You could read in Alpha for as long as your concentration span lasts. Some people's concentration span is five minutes, some people's is two minutes, some people's 20 minutes, and sometimes longer, it depends how thoroughly absorbing the information is. (How long are you in Alpha when you watch a good movie?)

Alpha is really easy to achieve. In fact, you use it all the time. It's the day dreaming state. It's the state of imagination. Kids from 0 to 5 live in this wonderful state. That's why they learn so much and do it with a very short concentration span. They absorb all information like a sponge, going straight to the subconscious mind. How quickly can you get into Alpha? Say you want to watch a fantastic movie, one that you really have been looking forward to. The movie is just starting; you turn on the TV. Before you get back to your seat and sit down — guess what? — you're in

the Alpha state. In other words you are only focused on the TV. You don't hear your wife (or your husband – I don't want to be sexist) speak to you. Have you ever seen kids watching television? They don't hear what you say – they're

HOW FAST YOU CAN GET INTO ALPHA

just totally focused on the television. Single focus, they're in the Alpha state. That's how easy it is! When watching a movie, or reading a thoroughly absorbing book, you are probably in the Alpha state. It's very easy!

Do this quick exercise. This is an example of how quickly you can get into – and out of – Alpha. I would like you to ... think of your mother's maiden name ...... Got it? Now, the second thing I want you to think of is ... a place that you'd love to go to, that perhaps you've never been to, but are yearning to go to – it is an idyllic place. When you get there you are going to have so much fun. Picture that beautiful place, and get an image of what it is like, in your mind. Have you got it?

Do you know that when you accessed your mother's maiden name, you were only thinking about that one thing. For that one fraction of a second you were in the Alpha state. Generally speaking there are other differences between the

Alpha state and the Theta state. However besides the number of cycles per second the main difference is that you actually lose the feeling in your body when you're in the Theta state. It takes about 15 minutes to get to Theta. People who practise daily meditation would be able to get there in 10 or 15 minutes, sometimes a little bit faster. Your mind is totally aware, totally in control, you can think quite clearly, but, you can't feel your body in the Theta state. In the Alpha state you know exactly where your body is. In both states you're in total control at all times.

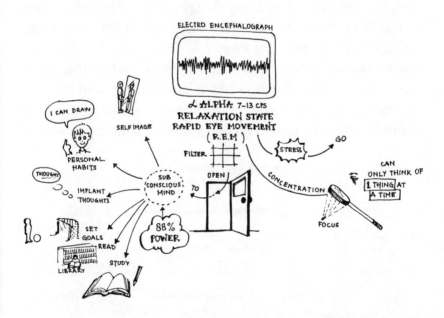

Let's talk about the Alpha state again. Stress reduction is one of the first things that can take place when using Alpha. The second thing is focused concentration. You focus or laser beam your mind; you listen to, or look at, or think about one thing at a time. That's focused concentration. Alpha opens up your mind to creativity and problem solving abilities. If you want to change your automatic pilot, change your personality, or the way you think and feel about yourself — your self-image, then this is the state in which you can do that, and feel better about yourself.

Beta State

I will move on to speak about the Beta state now. This is the beautiful, wide awake, logical thinking state, where we have divided attention. How many things can we think of at once in the Beta state? As adults we can think of five, six, seven, eight, or nine things at a time. It's just as well too, because when you are driving down the highway and you've got a truck on one side of you, a bus in front of you and another vehicle on the other side, and someone behind is trying to overtake you; the radio's on and someone's talking to you —

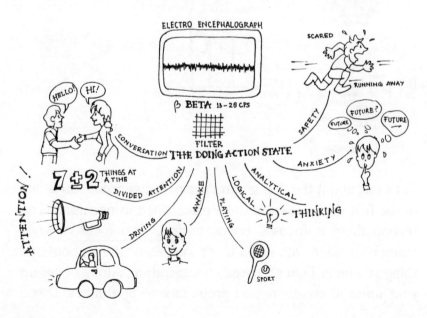

then you need to think of four, five, six, seven, eight things at a time don't you? Being in the Beta state can keep you safe. I certainly know that in conditions of say warfare, you really want to know who's in front of you, who's behind you, who's to the left, who's to the right, what should I be thinking about, where's this, what's that up there, planes flying, artillery firing, etc. To survive, you need to know and think about so many different things at once. So the Beta state is a very powerful state — it's the awake state, it's the divided attention state. It is the logical, analytical, action state, it's the state of doing. This is the state to be in to get things done. But, what does it create? — stress! This is the state in which stress occurs and increases. Sometimes our body releases that stress (unless we use an alarm clock, or recycle the bad things we might watch on television or some such similar thing). Beta state is the state in which stress occurs and accumulates unless we can let it go.

Examples of Alpha

So now I've talked about Delta, Theta, Alpha and Beta states. Alpha is the state of greatness and I'd like to just give you some more examples. Alpha was first used by Olympic athletes in 1964 — and the country using Alpha at that time was East Germany. In 1968 both Russia and East Germany were training their Olympic athletes in the Alpha state. In 1988 every country on the planet earth that sent people to the Olympic Games trained their athletes in the Alpha state.

The Sports Institute in Canberra teaches our sports men and

women to access the Alpha state. Top golfers use Alpha. Before they putt, before every swing, they physically go into Alpha very quickly and visualise themselves making the perfect shot.

Recently I read about a footballer saying over and over in his mind: "black dot, black dot, black dot, black dot, black dot." It was reported that you could just about see his lips muttering every time he was about to take a placement kick for a goal. It was like an "anchor" which meant to him that with single focused concentration in the Alpha state, "black dot" signified a perfect run up, a perfect kick, with the ball sailing over between the cross bars. (Later in the book I  will help you to develop an "anchor"). In fact entire football teams use mind training to win — they are all trained in the Alpha state. All top sportsmen and women and sports psychologists now know that when all physical attributes are equal, it is the mental preparation that makes the difference between winning and losing.

Another example: Thomas Edison was the most prolific inventor of our times. In fact he had 1,078 inventions of which over 1,000 are commercialised and used. Edison used to sit on a seat, with a stone pressed between his knees and underneath the stone there was a tin plate. He would go into the Alpha state, and the Theta state, and ask his subconscious mind to solve problems. He would feed in the problem and get an answer, which he would quickly write down. Then he would repeat the process. This is the main inspirational state in which he worked. Now, why did he have a stone between his knees? So that when he went into Delta (sleep) it dropped into the tin pan and woke him up of course. In the Delta state you can't think of a thing — you can't work in the Delta state — that's the deep sleep state. However, you can work in Alpha and you can work in Theta, and of course this happens in complete relaxation and focused concentration.

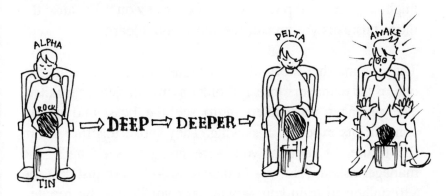

Edison conducted over 11,000 experiments to make a light bulb. After he had done about 5,000 experiments, and before he perfected a light bulb, a reporter asked him how he coped with so much failure. (Edison at that stage was regarded as a crank — the mad professor). What he was reported to have said was: "That's not failure, I just invented 5,000 different ways NOT to make a light bulb!" It's so true, positive language makes such a difference. Otherwise how could he have persevered? He did not regard his attempts as failure, rather as stepping stones to success.

HEY, I'VE JUST INVENTED 5,000 DIFFERENT WAYS OF NOT TO MAKE A LIGHT BULB

EDISON

Incidentally there was a very wealthy industrialist who was asked the secret of his success, and what would be his advice to others to be successful. His answer was: "Double your mistake rate!" What a great answer — different to what one might expect — step out of your Comfort Zone! Because the more mistakes you make, the more you'll learn.

There is another story about a General Manager who had one of his managers lose $10 million on a project that failed. The manager was called in to see the boss, and all his compatriots expected a sacking. They spoke together about the future. "I thought you were going to sack me?" the manager asked. "No way in the world — you've just cost me $10 million to train you — why sack you?" was the reputed retort. What a refreshing view and indeed a fantastic example for encouragement to all managers. Look at it positively, because it can be a big lesson. Mistakes can be stepping stones. It can be good to make mistakes — a shift in attitude can really help.

Remember comfort zones — you really don't learn a lot in your comfort zone. It's when you go through the barriers of doubt and fear and get **outside** your comfort zone, where you are **un**comfortable, that's where you can learn a lot. What can you easily do when you are out there, outside your comfort zone? – make some mistakes, sure – and that's OK, because that is how you learn. So turn mistakes into stepping stones.

Another example was Einstein. In his latter years Einstein lived on Princeton University Campus. He did much of his work in the Alpha state and often walked at the same time; whilst walking in the Alpha state he would get lost. To encourage Einstein to keep walking and working (disputing the quantum theory when he died at 76 years of age) they installed telephone booths all over the campus. When he came back to Beta, he would go to the nearest telephone, call and say "Hey guys I've done it again – please come and get me." They would ask him what number booth he was in, then send a vehicle to pick him up.

Examples of What to Do in Alpha

✦   "Reprogram" attitudes
✦   Study
✦   Play sports
✦   Read – and read much faster
✦   Achieve goals
✦   Achieve more sales, etc.

The information you need to retain and recall goes into the subconscious mind, where your memory is, when in Alpha.

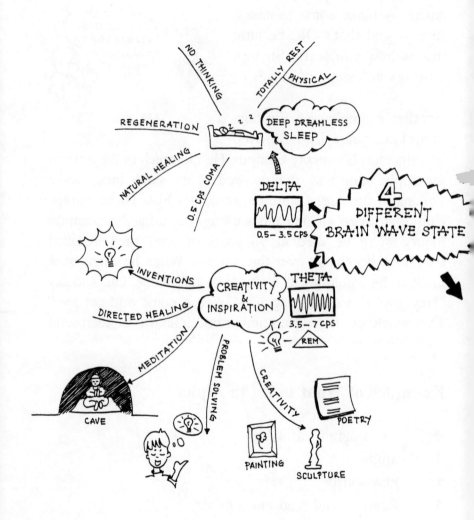

REVIEW OF CHAPTER 5

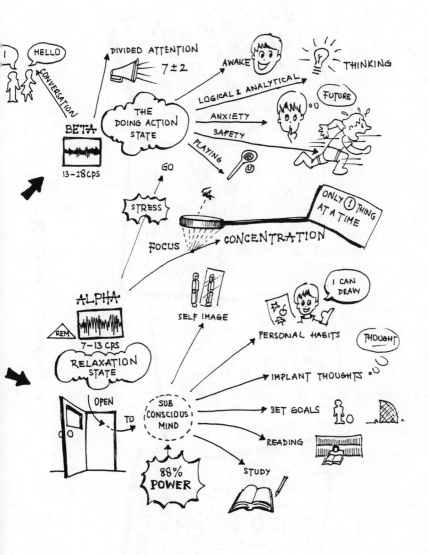

PREVIEW OF CHAPTER 6

6

THE RETICULAR ACTIVATING SYSTEM (RAS)

The Filter of the Reticular Activating System

You know that feeling when you're in an exam and want to recall some information. You know that you know the information, but you panic and can't think of the answer — you're in Beta, the stressful state. When you are stressed the Reticular Activating System (RAS) filter between your conscious and subconscious minds, closes tightly. The inform-

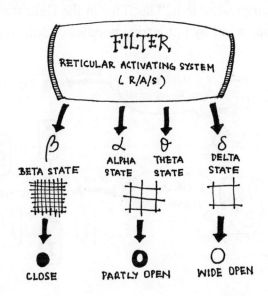

ation is right on the tip of your tongue, but you just can't get it! What happens ten minutes later, after the exam when you've relaxed? You can easily remember the name of the prime minister of Australia or Canada or whatever? The information just comes back to you, because you're relaxed. The filter stays tightly closed when you're stressed and in Beta. Next time you are doing an exam you will know how to relax (by going into Alpha) and access your memory when you need it most.

The filter in the Beta state is tightly closed. This is represented by the lines in the diagram on the previous page, which are close together. That filter is part of the Reticular Activating System and what it does is filter out information that you either don't need to know, or don't want to know. Do you know your mind is capable of remembering the shape of every grain of sand? It is capable of remembering every car that you pass on the road — but do you want to know these things? No of course not! So your mind filters this out, you're not interested in it. This filter in the Beta state actually protects your mind by not letting needless, cluttering inform-

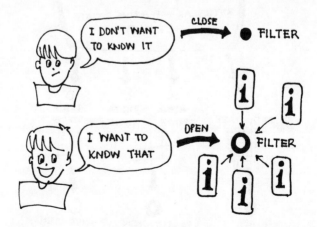

ation into your memory. You need to tell yourself that you are interested in certain information before the filter will cooperate. More of how we can use it soon.

When you're in either the Alpha or the Theta state the filter is partly open. When the filter is partly open it lets information into the memory bank. When you are learning, focusing on information, and you tell yourself "I want to know this", and when you say "I enjoy learning this" the emotion of this thought strengthens the imprinting of the information. The filter opens up and the information goes into that part of your subconscious mind, to that part of the memory bank, from which you will be able to access the information again. The Alpha and Theta states, are the relaxed single focus concentration states. You only think about what it is you're doing "right now" when you're in the Alpha and Theta states, and that's when information goes into the memory bank. Alpha is also the state to be in to recall information, that is when the filter is partly open, to let the information out.

In the Delta state the filter is wide open; and when it's wide open all information can enter, but, do you retain it? No (and here's another new piece of information) because the subconscious mind is a bit like the mind of a child, to operate effectively, the subconscious mind has to be controlled by the conscious mind. When you're in the Delta state the conscious mind is switched off and therefore it's only the subconscious mind in control. Remember the subconscious mind is a bit like the mind of a child and needs clear and specific direction. Children are not interested in something boring — they want to have fun.

Safety

Now what **can** happen in the Delta state is safety consciousness, which **can** be turned on by your "child like", simple, straightforward subconscious. Children, in their own minds, are very safety conscious most of the time. An example of the subconscious mind being alert to safety issues is if a mother has a baby in a room down the other end of the hallway from her own, and it makes a little whimper — guess what happens? A mother, or a father, can be roused from a deep, deep sleep by that little whimper, to go and attend to the baby. The subconscious mind, with the "mind of a child" directing it, hears the cry as a safety issue, to make sure the baby is all right. You've all heard of (or perhaps remember for yourself) a mother being woken from deep sleep by her child crying and the father sleeping through? Well, what can happen is that the father can either turn on to or off from the child's cries. When the eldest of my younger two children, was born, what happened was that my wife was particularly tired of course, and so I offered to be the one to get up and see that the baby was all right. But what happened was that Sandra would come padding along right behind me as well. I said: "This is crazy for both of us to be woken up by this little child, either you sleep through because you want to sleep, or you go to her and I'll stay asleep – I'm only doing it to help you get some more sleep." She said she was going to get up every time, so I said that in that case I would stay asleep, and I did – I just tuned out and I didn't hear the crying.

In fact, quite amazingly you can tune out to even louder noises. When I was in Vietnam in 1965 we had "long toms" which had about a 10m gun barrel (that's a huge barrel), firing shells which went 20,000 metres into the jungle. When they were being fired they shook the whole ground around us and they were being fired every hour, all night while we were in base camp. Why? – To keep the enemy awake and to keep them on the move – just to frustrate the enemy. Well believe you me after the first three or four days of this I thought "The sooner we get out into the bush away from these guns, the better". Well, after the first week or so we never heard those guns; they still kept firing, but the "child" controlling the subconscious mind recognised no danger, and we could sleep right through. The mind switched off because it was quite safe. So that's one good example of the value of this filter.

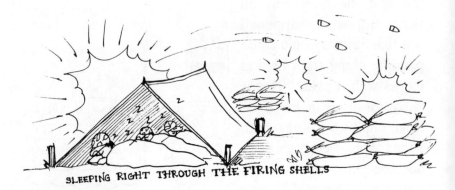

SLEEPING RIGHT THROUGH THE FIRING SHELLS

Using the RAS

Let's say you want to buy a 1971 red Maserati, although you have never actually seen a real one before. What you do is start telling yourself "I really want a 1971 Maserati". Amazingly, what happens is that you will see a Maserati drive past, you will see one in a garage, you will hear someone talking about it, you will start to see pictures of it in the newspaper. Your mind is switched on to whatever you tell yourself you want or need to know, so your filter opens up to the information that you need or want to know; even in the Beta state, the wide awake state. I'm sure you've been able to do it with something like a refrigerator for instance. If you really want a particular type of refrigerator at a particular price, you firstly start to think about it, telling yourself what you want. Suddenly you will be hearing about available refrigerators all over the place and you'll be able to have a choice of three or four. But up until now, you have never been

interested in refrigerators and so your mind wasn't activated to noticing the information relevant to that particular item. It was activated by telling yourself that you were interested in buying a refrigerator.

How can this be applied to your work? If you tell yourself for example "I'm not interested in chemistry, I hate chemistry" then when you're studying chemistry that filter will not let the information through. But there is a way of tricking the subconscious mind and tricking ourselves a little bit so that we are able to arouse our interest in information that we're not interested in. We'll learn about that soon. Once we have aroused interest then the filter of the Reticular Activating System will do its work and let in "chemistry" for example to the memory bank.

Relaxation

What do some of us do to relax? Read, listen to music, play sport, go for a run, bounce on the trampoline, work in the

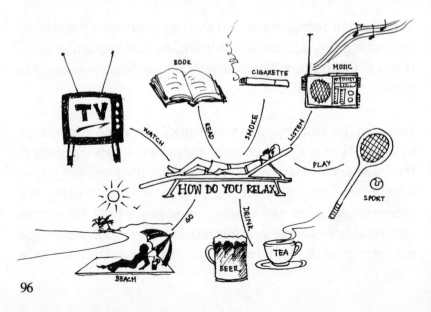

garden, have a swim, watch a movie, dance, go to a party, have a drink, or a cup of tea or coffee, a cigarette, food — people relax in lots of different ways. If you have "told" yourself that doing a certain thing will calm you down, make you feel relaxed, then that idea forms inside your sub-conscious mind, (this is part of your self image) and tells you that every time you do that certain thing you will feel calm and relaxed. Your subconscious mind takes over and that is precisely what does happen. (Many times you can convince yourself you are relaxing, for instance by having a cigarette, and yet your pulse rate actually increases, so that's NOT real relaxation).

Some other things that people do to relax is to just do nothing, just sit and daydream, which is partly what "going into the Alpha brainwave state to achieve relaxation" is about.

Music

Music used for relaxation and study is music that is 56 to 64 beats to the minute. Music, with 56 beats to the minute, can have the effect of "getting your heart beat in time with the music". It can actually slow down your heart beat to 56 to 64 beats per minute. Now when your heart beat slows down you are moving towards being in the Alpha state, so you can help yourself to get into (and stay in) Alpha, by using music.

For studying and learning now, baroque music is often used, which has 60 beats per minute, in four/four time. The idea is

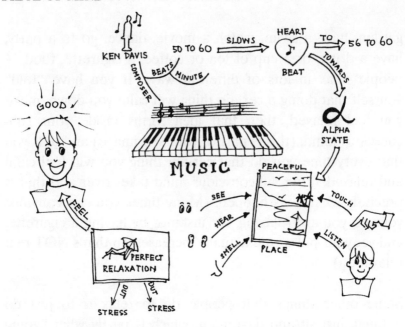

to have the music playing in the background so that your heart beat slows down to be in time with the music and when that happens you're actually going to the Alpha state, to that relaxation state. (See page 234).

An important point to note here is that to some people music can be a distraction — a very small percentage, but if you're one of that small percentage, then recognise that and turn the music off. You can do it without the music. Generally speaking most people are musical and they just "go off with the music". Just a word about artists and creators, and in particular: Ken Davis, the artist who created my music called *Infinite Joy*. When Ken Davis creates music he's actually in the meditative state. He goes to play his piano, which has a tape recorder built into it, and whilst he is in a state of meditation he plays, but doesn't even know what he's played. It's automatically recorded though, so that then he can come back and listen to that music again just to see how inspirational it is. That's one way Ken Davis uses the relaxed state. Many famous artists have used this state for many, many creative endeavours.

Letting Go

I'd like now to illustrate the difficulty nearly all of us have in letting go of embedded belief patterns. It is a story about how monkeys are caught by the indigenous people of Borneo. They use a coconut, a piece of string and a peanut. One end of the coconut is cut open and a peanut is put inside. The other end is tied to a piece of string. The monkey is attracted to the moving coconut, spies the peanut inside, puts a hand

into the coconut and fastens onto the peanut. The hand is now a fist, firmly grasping the peanut. However the fist is now bigger than the opening of the coconut. The monkeys go crazy dancing around to shake off the coconut. They stomp on it and hit it against their head, all to no avail. Do they let go of the peanut? No! In fact the monkey gets caught and gives up its life rather than let go of the peanut.

How many "peanuts" do we hang onto? How many "peanuts" do we never let go of? How many things do we hang onto in life that no longer serve us? You are now going to have an opportunity to challenge your belief system and work with an exercise in guided imagery.

Questions and Answers

When you're actually in Alpha and Theta, can you tell, and how do you know?

Yes, you can tell and one way to tell is for someone else to observe your rapid eye movement (REM). Sometimes you can feel your own REM. You will know when you're in the Theta state because you actually do not feel your body (it's as though it's numb) yet you have total control and your mind is extremely lucid. The other mechanical way is by measuring your brain waves with the electro-encephalograph (or other devices designed for this purpose). There is a much more practical way however, which I will introduce after you get to Alpha.

Which would be the better state in which to control pain?

The Theta state is a better state to use for controlling pain, but it can also be done in the Alpha state. Care must be taken with use of language, because pain is a signal that something is wrong with our body; it is necessary to find out what causes that pain. It's the hurt that is in the pain that can be released.

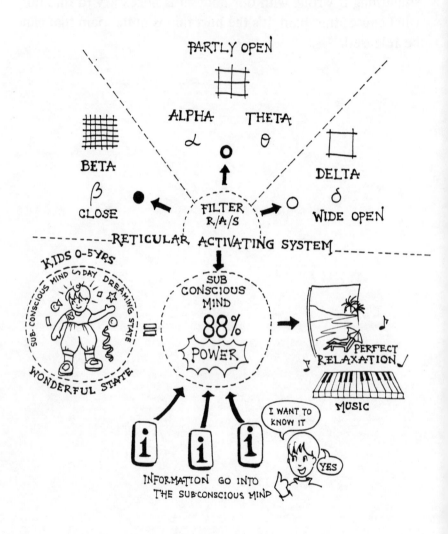

REVIEW OF CHAPTER 6

*Relax to recall –
relaxation opens the
reticular activating filter and
you get direct access to the
subconscious mind – that is,
to your memory*

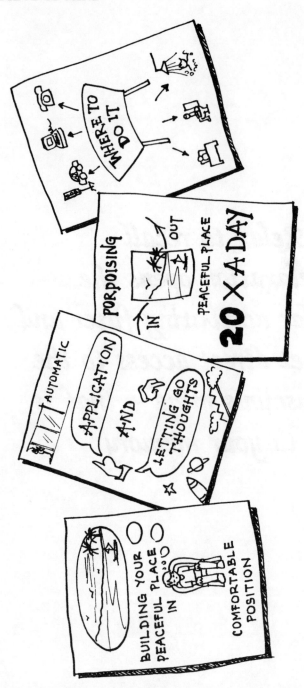

PREVIEW OF CHAPTER 7

7

BUILDING YOUR PEACEFUL PLACE

I have produced a guided imagery music tape called *A Peaceful Place No. 2 – (Guided Imagery)*, with the music *Infinite Joy* composed by Ken Davis, which you can use – or you can make your own tape. (In the **Peaceful Place** series, *A Peaceful Place No. 1* is just instrumental.) What my voice does in the guided imagery is to take you on a journey. The journey is to a place inside your mind, to a place of relaxation whereby you have total control. A place where you know that you've had perfect relaxation at one time during your life. You bring it back in visual, auditory and kinesthetic words. So you feel it, you smell it, you touch it, you hear it, and you see it inside your mind. You relive the sensation of relaxation. From this place of relaxation a magic pathway opens up. You go along this pathway (all inside your mind) to a place that can either be a place of reality or imagination, which we call your "Peaceful Place" – a place where you have perfect peace – even more relaxation than you have experienced in your relaxed place that you just relived inside your mind. This Peaceful Place that you create is a place inside your mind which is so relaxed that every time you gain access to your Peaceful Place you have automatic relaxation and stress goes. You in fact are going to be the architect, the designer, the builder — of this place inside your own mind. So firstly you'll build the floor, then the walls and the ceiling, the outside, the inside — all of this will be done in your own mind. It can be a place you have actually been to, or it can be a place completely created by your imagination. Your ultimate aim is to be able to get to that Peaceful Place inside your mind in a few seconds, and this you will be able to do, with practice. Every time you access it, relaxation is automatic and stress goes. So that's what will happen.

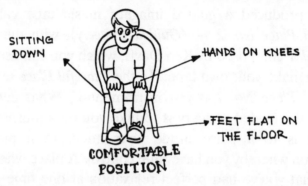

SITTING DOWN

HANDS ON KNEES

FEET FLAT ON THE FLOOR

COMFORTABLE POSITION

Now before you start you need to be in what is called a comfortable position. Sitting down in a chair with your feet flat on the floor is probably the best position. My advice to you is to put your hands on your knees. Some of you will be able to do this in yoga positions and if you are used to doing yoga and would like to do that, then that's fine. But for most of you, if you do that, or if you cross your legs or arms, then what can happen is that the blood flow can stop and you may feel pins and needles or even a little twinge of pain. Of course when that happens you're in the Beta state — you're thinking of two things at a time, because being aware of the pain distracts you. Therefore make sure you feel comfortable, with no tight clothing.

There are three steps to building your Peaceful Place. The initial step of creating your Peaceful Place will take about twenty minutes. The next step is to get to your Peaceful Place taking only three minutes. The third step is to practise what is called "porpoising". By the time you finish these three steps you will be actually accessing your Peaceful Place and releasing stress in 30 seconds. You see it's a process that anyone can use (especially busy people) at any time to release stress in thirty seconds.

Building Your Peaceful Place

For those of you who have bought my tape, *A Peaceful Place No. 2 (Guided Imagery)*, play it until you have completed the first section (you will recognise when this is). Remember to allow yourself 20 minutes of quiet, uninterrupted time. For those of you who have not bought the tape, you could make your own tape, preferably with background music of 56 beats to the minute, saying the same words that I have said (see the transcript on the next page) and then play this, your own tape, to yourself.

The following is a transcript of side one of my tape, using guided imagery to build your own Peaceful Place, a place where relaxation is automatic and stress goes.

First, get into a comfortable position — a good idea is to sit in a chair with your feet flat on the floor — your hands resting on your thighs. Now ... take a deep breath ..... And let it all out...... And take another deep breath in, feeling it going right down to your abdomen and ... this time ... let out any tensions and anxieties as you breathe out. Let them all go. And now, softly breathe in and gently .. close .. your .. eyes....... and as you listen to the sound of my voice, you follow along the guidance offered ... .. with the music in the background, knowing at all times that you and you alone are in control .... Now in your mind .... seek and find .... a relaxed place ..... a relaxed place that you know that you've been to before ... and there you had such perfect relaxation ...... now in your mind .... rebuild that scene .... using your five senses ...... first of all .... bring in all the sights .... that are around you .... are you in the open .... is there green grass ..... are there flowers .... is there a forest ..... are you on a mountain top ..... is there snow ..... or are you inside a house ... or a special place .....see what's around you... and now recall and hear the sounds ..... can you hear any wind .... or ocean ... or water .... is anybody saying anything to you ..... and now you just get a sense of that place ..... like touching ..... and feeling ... and smelling ... all the things that are around ..... and from your relaxed place .... you look around ..... and you either get the sense of, or you see or you feel yourself being drawn to a magic pathway ..... it's a pathway that's just opening up ..... and leading off .... it's a pathway that's just opening up .... and leading off ..... where is it leading to ..... is it going up in the air ..... is it going to mountain tops ..... is it going across the sea .... is it going to another universe ..... is it going through parks and gardens .... or forests ..... and as you feel yourself being drawn along this magic pathway .... you go ... because you know .... whatever is at the end of this pathway ... is just so real for you ..... so wonderful .. so magical .... because it is your Peaceful Place ..... you are the architect .... you are the builder .. and you are the owner of this Peaceful Place ..... and every time you get to this Peaceful Place ..... you are relaxed ..... and stress goes .....

You start building your Peaceful Place by deciding on the floor
.... what is it made of ..... is the floor in fact grass ..... or is it
timber ... or is it cloud ..... is it air ..... is it glass ..... whatever it
is you build it ... so do that now ..... and now you build the
walls ... in the same way ..... you choose the material ... do you
have any walls ..... or is it out in the open ..... whatever it is you
choose the material and you build it .... and now you build
the roof in the same way ..... do you have a roof or .... are the
stars your roof ..... is a canopy of trees your roof ... or glass .....
or tile or timber ..... whatever it is you build it .... and now
inside your Peaceful Place .... you look outside .... you may need
to put in windows ... so you do that .... and as you look
outside you put in all the scenery ... that you either see or you
want to see... from your Peaceful Place... so whatever it is, you
do that, right around you.... and now, inside ... your Peaceful
Place ... you put in all the things that you really want with you
... what are they? Do you have your favourite furniture, your
favourite pictures? Do you bring in your favourite hobby?
Whatever it is ... you bring in, and decorate your Peaceful Place.
And now, in your Peaceful Place, you place a chair ... do you
sit on a special chair ... something that's soft that you sink right
into ... or do you sit on the ground, or the floor. This magical
chair, it has so many wonderful powers for you. Every time you
sit in it, you know that relaxation has begun, and that stress
goes ... and you're able to do anything you want in this magical
chair ... So now you stand up, and you walk through the
entrance of your Peaceful Place ... you give yourself some sort
of combination, or some sort of switch, some sort of sign
perhaps, or some sort of word you use, to gain entry into your
Peaceful Place. So as you exit, you look back, knowing exactly
how you gain entry. Do you press a button? Or is it your body
that just lets you through. And so now you move down the

magical pathway, knowing that at any time you will be able to get back to your Peaceful Place, and that any time that you get back there, relaxation has begun, and stress goes. ... So as you move down your magical pathway, you move into the first place you started from, which was your relaxed place, so that once again you become familiar with it .... What is there around you ......what do you see and hear and feel? .... And now from your relaxed place you return to the present.... on the count of 5, you're going to open your eyes.

And when you do, you will be relaxed and alert and well, and invigorated, and ... you will know that you will be able to get back to your Peaceful Place at any time, and when you do, you have relaxation, and stress goes. ... so on the count of ONE, you can feel the blood flowing to your fingers and your toes ... on the count of TWO, you move your fingers and toes a little bit, and THREE, you stretch your body a little bit ... and FOUR, you just roll your neck ... and FIVE, your eyes open, wide awake, alert, well, healthy and invigorated, knowing that you can get back to your Peaceful Place at any time.

Exercise

*It is very important to describe and recreate your Peaceful Place using different learning skills and involving the use of different intelligences (see Chapter 13), and it is now time to do that. The first thing is to describe your Peaceful Place out loud. You could choose to describe it to someone else and get them to describe it back to you — you see you may want to **hear** the description, or if you don't want to do that you could describe* *it by recording onto a cassette. For some people it's very important to hear what that Peaceful Place is about — that's their way of learning. Or for others it's very important for them to talk about it and say — "This is what I did, this is where it was, it was so beautiful" — and to describe it maybe by using hands and very descriptive adjectives. Now what I would like you to do is to take a pencil and write in the space provided below, all about your Peaceful Place. Be as descriptive as you possibly can. Read it out aloud to yourself, and if you would like to, you can then record it onto a cassette.*

....
....
....
....
....
....
....
....
....
....
....

The next part of the exercise for you to complete is to take a piece of paper and some coloured pencils or pens and draw your Peaceful Place. You can do this with your non-dominant hand, or even shut your eyes. It's not what it looks like that's important. You are helping to indelibly imprint your Peaceful Place into your memory, by the physical activity of drawing it.

Now tell yourself "Well done". How often do we tell ourselves "Well done"? This is very important for self image.

Discussion About Your Peaceful Place

There may be a few things we might need to clear up about the Peaceful Place. Let's say for example your Peaceful Place is a place of total imagination. Your Peaceful Place may have turned out to be your first relaxed place; the magic path may have turned right around and came straight back to the relaxed place — that's absolutely fine, because that means that your relaxed place is important to you.

Now what is really important is that you only have one Peaceful Place — just one. You can't have two or three or four. When you stub your toe and you really hurt it and want to relieve the hurt, you don't want to think "Hey which

Peaceful Place do I go to?" With practice you will develop a neural pathway to the one Peaceful Place. You want to go straight there and to know it exactly and you'll start relieving the hurt straight away. It's an automatic action. It becomes

automatic. We only have one Peaceful Place, — the one that you are going to work with today and always. Now you can change it and rebuild it, that's okay. If you want to change it, alter it or rebuild it, that's fine.

For instance, how many of you have someone there with you in your Peaceful Place? That is OK, as long as it's all right with you. What's important is that you are in total control and you can ask them to leave (and make sure that they do leave), at any time, or invite them in if you wish. So just say in your mind "leave", if that's what you want. Do you actually see your Peaceful Place, very clearly visualised? Do you just get a sense that there's something there? That's the way it is for me. I don't see a thing and I've been imagining for years. Sandra, my wife, sees things so easily, but for me I just say "I know it's there". There may be a black hole but then in my mind I say "it's there". If that's the way it is for you then that's fine.

Now if you want people to come in and be your adviser, or your teacher, or if there's someone else you want to be involved with, then ask them in and say "I want to ask you some questions" — and then get some answers. You can do this all in your own imagination. The key thing is that you control it. You are the boss, so you are in control. You can bring in photos, precious belongings, anything at all that you like.

Your Peaceful Place in Three Minutes

You have completed a process that took about 20 minutes to do. You are going to do it again, taking only three minutes. Once again, it is better to listen to the music tape with my voice to go back to your Peaceful Place, only much quicker, and then come back again. The reason you are doing this is to gradually establish a neural pathway to that same Peaceful Place. Eventually you want to get there in a few seconds and release stress each time. It just takes you a few seconds, then relaxation and releasing stress become automatic. Sometimes you can do it with your eyes open, but if you prefer, then keep your eyes closed, to eliminate distractions. Firstly you need to establish this neural pathway by going to your Peaceful Place many times. Eventually it will be instantaneous. So now, in three minutes.

Once again, the first step is to get into a comfortable position. Preferably uncross legs and arms and hands, unless of course you really don't want to, because there are no absolute hard and fast rules — you do what you feel most comfortable with. In fact you are your own GURU. Do you know how I spell GURU? — Gee - yoU - aRe - yoU.

Now play the next part of *A Peaceful Place No. 2 — (Guided Imagery)*, (until you open your eyes) or make your own tape using the following words.

Let's just take a deep breath ... now let it all out ...take another deep breath, and gently close your eyes. ... And once again, in your mind, find that magical Peaceful Place ... that calming scene that you built yourself ....inside your mind. Find that quiet restfulness, that peacefulness, that oneness, and imagine so much calmness, as you now are totally relaxed. See....or pretend to see ....hear or pretend to hear ....feel or pretend to feel..... your quiet Peaceful Place. Just pretend that you're really in your Peaceful Place. See the scenes that are around you, and hear the lovely restful sounds. Hear the calming music, it aids and comforts you. An abundance of warmth and flow of good feelings are in your Peaceful Place. And so easily you can return to your Peaceful Place where you're in the Alpha brain wave state..... You do it so easily — straight to your Peaceful Place. ... Now, on the count of five you will once again open your eyes and you will be relaxed, well, healthy and invigorated. ONE, TWO, you just start moving your fingers, THREE you stretch a little bit, FOUR you roll your neck, and FIVE, eyes open, wide awake, relaxed, well, healthy and invigorated.

Further Discussion

I hope most of you managed to get back to your Peaceful Place. If you didn't, where did you go, was it somewhere else? Remember I said before that we're not responsible for all our thoughts. One thing for sure is that thoughts will always come, so here's a couple of suggestions as to what to do with thoughts. One is that you just watch the thought come in, treat them as things — thoughts are things — watch them come in and watch them go out. If necessary picture a clothesline and hang out your thoughts and then shoot them away from you. Put them on a never ending escalator and let them go. Attach them to an aeroplane flying overhead. Some of my seminar participants have ended up in the aircraft —

then they're in another universe, or on holiday in Bali — in other words, they just haven't let go of the thought, but have pursued another thought. Whatever is a good way for you to let go of your thoughts, then do it. If you hang on to the thought then what happens is that you will find you follow that thought through and get taken off the track of being in your Peaceful Place.

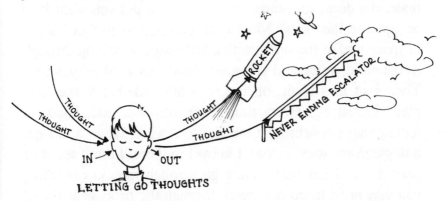

You're still in the Alpha state as you follow that thought, but what you need to do then, if this does happen, is to tell yourself to come back to your Peaceful Place. Sometimes, at first, some of you will need to go along your magical pathway or even to come from your relaxed place and from there go back to your Peaceful Place. Some of you can simply say: "Back to Peaceful Place" and you just go back there in your mind.

So, whatever thoughts come through to you, just make it okay, that's important. Thoughts sometimes are going to come, so you make it okay, recognise them and take control. What you do is just let them go. Just as they come in, let them go out, treat them as things, waves through the atmosphere, coming in and going out again, in the left ear and out the right.

Now for those who did not get to their Peaceful Place, have you actually created it in your mind? Were you the architect, did you build it, did you physically tell yourself in your own mind that you could see things in your mind? Or if you couldn't do that, did you get a sense of it? A sense of the floor, the door, the shape, the roof — or did you want it to be open to the skies? Mine is in the open — in fact it's out in space and in the open, with a little stream flowing through it, coloured water and coloured clouds, as vivid as possible. Then I sit in a chair, on top of a hill and that is the final place I'm sitting. Every time I get into that seat, I have a feeling that goes through me like — a whooosh — and I get a tingle in my toes — then I know I'm there. I don't see it or hear it, but I get that feeling go through me. So one thing you may need to do is to work through the process again, of creating your Peaceful Place. Do it in your imagination — you don't have to see it. Before you start to replay your tape (the 20 minute version) just make sure that in doing so, you make whatever happens okay. Know and acknowledge that what's happening is that you're going to rebuild your Peaceful Place, that you go there from your relaxed place, along a magic pathway.

Some of you may need a little bit more time than three minutes to get to your Peaceful Place. You might need to do it in say four minutes to start with, but eventually you will get that feeling that you are there. Make yourself comfortable about it because the time that the process takes is different for everyone. So for those of you that need to — just do the three minute tape again.

I can now get to my Peaceful Place in a few seconds — but I've been doing it for a while. It depends on how many times you do it .... everybody needs to practise at least 20 times a day for say a month. Now that 20 times a day is 10 minutes a day, thirty seconds at a time, going through the whole cycle. You want it to be so automatic that it's like driving a car. When you're driving a car and another car comes across the road in front of you, what do you automatically do? What's your first action? Put your foot on the brake. Do you really think about it? Do you really think about: "Oh, a car in front of me. What do I do now? Do I brake? How do I do that, do I use the left foot or the right foot, or should I use the hand brake?" You don't think about it do you? It becomes so automatic that you just put your foot on the brake. That's as automatic as this is going to be.

"Falling" Asleep

Before you move on to the exercise of Porpoising one more element has to be introduced. After you take a deep breath, close your eyes and go to your Peaceful Place, you then raise your eyes up and lower them — (keeping your eyes shut). It's that simple, just raise your eyeballs up by pretending that you're looking at a spot on the ceiling overhead and then look straight ahead again (all with your eyes shut). Try it now: eyes up, and back to level again. The reason this is done is that you are tricking your mind into thinking you are going to sleep. What's the first stage in going to sleep? The first stage is to go to the Alpha state (the relaxed state). The second stage is to go to the Theta state (the dream state), and the third stage is to go to the Delta state (the deep sleep

state). The mind always goes through that process and what happens normally when you are asleep is that the eyes roll up. When the eyes are rolled up, they rest behind the hardest bone in the body, which is the forehead. By the action of rolling up our eyes, what we are doing is tricking the mind, the mind thinks that we're on the way to sleep. It cooperates because we are — we're on the way to Alpha, but not to sleep, because the conscious mind knows to take control. It's a good trick.

Now some people of course don't go through Alpha and Theta to go to sleep, they go straight to Theta. Have you heard of people "falling" asleep? When they "fall asleep, the brainwave cycles go from 13 to 28 cycles per second down to 3½ to 7 cycles per second. What happens to their body when they're "falling" asleep is a little jerk. Have you ever felt yourself jerk — like a little kick — when you're falling asleep. That means that you are just going down so fast (brainwaves cycles go from 28 to 7 cycles per second) that your body responds with a little jerk or kick. And that's all it is, just your brain cycles per second changing very quickly.

Porpoising

We will now do **porpoising** — that is getting to your Peaceful Place in a few seconds, and remember each time you get to your Peaceful Place the automatic action is that you are relaxed and stress goes. Practise this for 10 minutes a day, for a month to make it a fantastic habit.

Now play the next part of *A Peaceful Place No. 2 (Guided Imagery)*; (this is the last part on side 1) or make your own tape, using the following words.

Get into a comfortable position ..... Take a deep breath and ....let it out. Now take another deep breath, and, close your eyes ... and go to your Peaceful Place. Roll your eyes up, and down, just for a fraction of a second ... and in your Peaceful Place, just pick up your surroundings once again. Feel and hear and see all that you need to — to know that you're in your Peaceful Place ... and take a deep breath, and open your eyes.

Now take another deep breath, and close your eyes, and go to your Peaceful Place, raise your eyes up, and down ... and once again become familiar with your surroundings ... now take a deep breath, and open your eyes ...

Now take another deep breath, close your eyes, and go to your Peaceful Place, ... roll your eyes up, and down ... take a deep breath and open your eyes.

Take a deep breath, and close your eyes ... go to your Peaceful Place ... roll your eyes up, and down ... and take a deep breath and open your eyes.

Discussion Again

Did you get back to your Peaceful Place? If you didn't, the first thing to do is, inside of you, make that okay, because you **will** get there, it just means you need a little bit more time and practice. Another way to get there is to go into your "relaxed place" first of all, then go along your magic pathway, then go to your Peaceful Place, and take just a little bit more time to get there. Generally speaking, it's the kinesthetic people (like me) who don't see or hear their Peaceful Place, but have a need to feel it, who take a little longer to realise that they in fact are there. Imagination really helps. Have you ever heard of "fake it till you make it"? It works — pretend that you're there. So just make it okay inside your mind and take a little bit more time in setting the scenery.

Another point that may effect you; some people don't need to do the action of rolling their eyes up and down because what happens is that their Peaceful Place, which they already see so clearly, disappears whenever they roll their eyes up. Has that happened to you? If it happened then don't roll your eyes up and down. This technique is so individual. Be your own GURU for relaxation.

The idea with porpoising is to make getting there an automatic action inside your mind and to do that, practise 20 times a day for a month. Now if a person chooses to do it one hundred times a day, and takes say 20 or 30 or 40

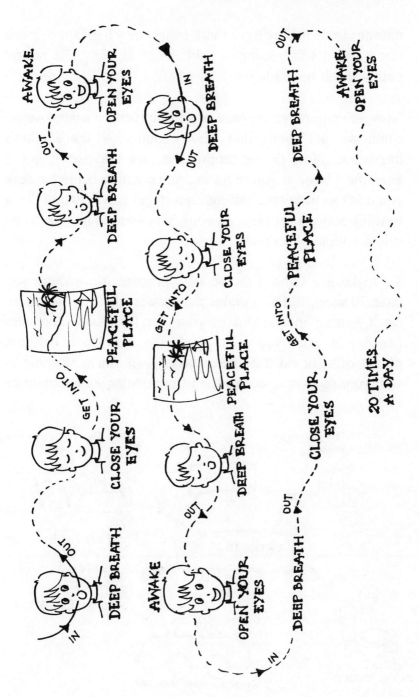

minutes to do it, they'll get there faster, they'll get there more often and it will become a habit more quickly. The neural pathway will be made.

Now we've done an exercise of getting there, it's what we do when we get there that really counts — that's what's important. How do we utilise the fact that we've got a Peaceful Place? If you're an executive sitting behind a desk you don't want to take five minutes to get to a Peaceful Place to think about a problem do you? You want to be able to do it in a couple of seconds.

To make it a habit, practise it ... practise it anywhere you have 30 seconds. Do it under the shower, do it on the toilet, do it getting in and out of your car (especially for sales people) or when you've stopped your car. Do it between phone calls, or do it between tasks — if you're wanting to shift your focus of concentration from one area to another or

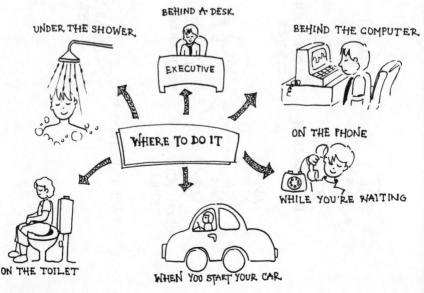

UNDER THE SHOWER

BEHIND A DESK

EXECUTIVE

BEHIND THE COMPUTER

WHERE TO DO IT

ON THE PHONE

WHILE YOU'RE WAITING

ON THE TOILET

WHEN YOU START YOUR CAR

from say a human resources problem to an operations problem, you just take 30 seconds and quickly relax, refocus. Practise, practise, practise — just do it!

Exercise

I would like you to take a break from reading this book and do the following:

1. *Practise 20 times going into your Peaceful Place then out again; going in and out — the complete cycle. This builds the neural pathway. For some of you that will take 10 minutes, and for others it will take less, or maybe even a bit longer.*

2. *Emotion is the language of the subconscious mind. It's an extremely important function of memory. This exercise is to think of some good experiences in your life. You need to bring back the feeling you had when you had that good experience, whether it be a feeling of floating or lightness; whether it be a shiver down your back or a warm glow. Whatever that particular feeling might be that you experience when you have a positive emotion during those good experiences is what you need to tap into. So please go back to three events in your life which are good, positive events and bring forward and recognise that physical feeling you had in your body. What is the sensation in your body? That's important.*

So do those things before you continue with the book.

How was that? Did you manage to get in 20 practices? I can tell you that if you don't do it, and keep on doing it and doing it, then it won't happen for you. If you don't do it you wont' do it and you'll never get it, ever. So it's entirely up to you. Doing it does it, there is no other way that you'll be able to get it.

What about the exercise of recapturing three occasions of emotions? Did any of you find it difficult? There's no doubt about getting to emotions, some people can bottle it up without even recognising what they are doing. This may be so much so in some cases, that getting back to an emotion can be a most difficult exercise. If that is the case for you, then it will be all right, because we will be doing another exercise whereby we will build a picture of what was the good scene surrounding that emotion. It is the feeling that we need to tap into. For the people who are not kinesthetic at all, then it may be more difficult.

Questions and Answers

I try so hard to get to my Peaceful Place — can you give me another tip?

Let me first mention what "trying" means. Do you know that to try, implies failure. Think of the action another way, either do it or don't do it, but don't "try" to do it. "Trying", to the subconscious mind, implies failure. Now for the tip: when you're anxious, go to your Peaceful Place through your relaxed place and then your magic pathway. You can do it very quickly. Another tip, start to go to your Peaceful Place after you have taken three deep breaths, saying the word "relax" as you breathe out.

When I go to my Peaceful Place I feel my eyes flickering, which can be distracting — is this normal?

It's normal but not many people have got such a great signal to tell them they are in Alpha. The flickering is the REM state (some people may want to feel it and you can do that by concentrating on your eyes). If it distracts you then let it be OK inside your mind and treat the information (of "my eyes are flickering") as a thought. Let the thought in and then let it out.

I'm not visual at all and therefore I don't think I have a Peaceful Place. What should I do?

I personally do not see anything in my Peaceful Place, at least not the same way I see in a dream. Many people do see it clearly, but mine just "looks like" a black hole. I imagine that I see my Peaceful Place and when I sit down in my magic chair I feel a wave of relaxation go through my body and that's my signal. Other people may hear wind or the sea when they get to their Peaceful Place. Keep practising, knowing that when you imagine you're checking out your Peaceful Place, you are then in Alpha. You may develop a signal which tells you for sure that you're in your Peaceful Place.

Can I get to my Peaceful Place when I'm stressed? How do I do it?

Two ways. You need to take longer in the early stages, ie. before Alpha is a habit; so go into your relaxed place, through the pathway to your Peaceful Place. The second way is to play my tape to yourself [*A Peaceful Place No. 2 (Guided Imagery)*].

I'm struggling between two Peaceful Places, how do I choose the right one?

Build it again. Use the tape *A Peaceful Place No. 2 (Guided Imagery)* side one. Whichever is dominant will come in to your mind first. If the other one comes in, ask yourself which Peaceful Place is best for you and then go with your intuition. If the second Peaceful Place is still around then treat it as a thought and just imagine that the thought goes out (in fact you are taking control of the thought).

What about people in my Peaceful Place? How do I "use" them or how do I let them go?

You must take control of the situation in your Peaceful Place. If you want people in or out you invite them in; you tell them to come in and stay, or to go out. If they persist and won't go, then build yourself another Peaceful Place. You can bring people in and seek their assistance and guidance by asking them questions. Try it, you'll find the power amazing.

Why do I need to go to my Peaceful Place twenty times a day for a month?

Because you are building a neural pathway to your Peaceful Place. The more often you do it, the faster you will get there (a couple of seconds) and the action of going there becomes automatic: as automatic as driving a car (you don't think about how to drive any more — it just happens).

When I am in my Peaceful Place and I get distracted in my mind, what do I do to get focused?

Sometimes your mind wanders — for instance when you're letting go of a thought by attaching it to an aeroplane, you can end up in the plane. Not only that, you might end up in Bali — where the plane lands. As soon as you catch yourself out and notice that your mind is wandering, just tell yourself "Come on back — back to my Peaceful Place and sit in the chair". It works for me and I'm sure it can work for you.

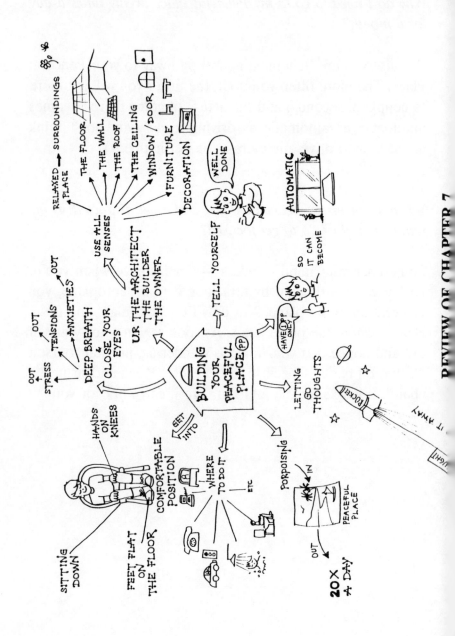

REVIEW OF CHAPTER 7

*When you do
guided imagery,
or visualise
inside your mind,
you do it by
sensing or
seeing or
feeling or
hearing or
smelling or
tasting or
talking to yourself
or any combination
of the above*

PREVIEW OF CHAPTER 8

8

THE LAWS AND LANGUAGE OF THE SUBCONSCIOUS MIND

Imagination and Reality

The most valuable piece of information that you put to use in this whole book is that *the subconscious mind does not know the difference between imagination and reality.* The subconscious mind has no mechanism for recognising what is real and what is not real.

As a quick example, let's take a dream and let's say that you're dreaming that you are being pursued — you're running away, you're in escape mode — in your dream. Your adrenalin is running, your heart's beating faster, you're really trying to get away. But what is the mechanism that tells you — "Hey everything's OK, I'm safe and not really being pursued at all"? The mechanism is the conscious mind, because you wake up and say "Whewww it was only a dream." The subconscious mind is having a dream and it can not tell the difference between reality and imagination, because it really thought someone or something was chasing you. You were being pursued, but then it was the conscious mind that recognised "Hey I'm not being pursued at all, it was only a dream — thank goodness."

So that really is the single most important point which you're going to be able to put to use because we can trick the subconscious mind into anything. Especially when we have something boring to do, we can even trick it into thinking that it's really interesting. That can be very handy, particularly when you've got to study chemistry and you hate chemistry, for example.

Laws of the Subconscious Mind

Now there are four "laws" of the subconscious mind and just to make it easy they all start with the letter "P".

Positive

The first "P" is for Positive. The language that you use to talk to the subconscious mind needs to be positive. What do you

think of when I say "Don't think of a rainbow? ... ...
You think of a rainbow! What do you think of when I say
"Don't worry"? Do you know what that means to the
subconscious mind? It means "Worry", and "Don't forget"
means "Forget".

I have often noticed on the TV, for example at the end of a
national news report, the announcer says something like: "...
don't forget the next program coming up is ....." If you say
"Don't forget" to the subconscious mind it means "Forget".

You say to your child "Johnny don't cross the road". Johnny
wasn't even thinking of crossing the road, but what has his
attention been drawn to and what is he thinking of now?
Crossing the road! Our language is extremely important
because the way we speak to ourselves and the way we speak
to other people can effect us a great deal, especially if we
allow it to, or if we are unaware of how to stop it from doing
so. Self talk creates habits which reside in our subconscious
mind. Self talk creates self esteem
which in turn creates self image,
which is in the subconscious mind.
Loving parents are the people that
really start this because they want
to save Johnny from an accident
when crossing the road. So, it can
start with loving parents, then
friends and school teachers,
because they also have a lot of
influence over us. The first law
then is positive self talk.

Present Tense

The second law is Present tense. I'll give you a good example of this. "I'm going on a diet tomorrow". What happens when the subconscious mind gets to tomorrow? Is it tomorrow yet? No, it's today, it's now, it's always "now" to the subconscious mind, never tomorrow. Always use the present tense — that's the second "P".

You can program future events. What you do is program the future (in your mind) as though it is NOW. For instance, let's say that you want to telephone a friend on their birthday; what you do is program yourself by seeing yourself,

and hearing yourself calling your friend in your mind **now, as though it is their birthday**. See yourself checking the calendar — seeing the highlighted date. Endeavour to make some other relevant association and then "make the call" inside your mind as though the birthday is **now**.

Personal

The third law is Personal. The language of the subconscious mind is the language of "I". Not you, they or or us — but **I**. Sometimes use your own name. I, Sandy MacGregor .... weigh 89 kilos on 16 March (that's my birthday) .... (and put the year). I achieve 93% in my final exams in .... (year). That's how you talk to your own subconscious mind with self talk.

Persistence

The fourth "P" is Persistence. Another word for persistence is repetition. How many times do you need to do it before the subconscious mind gets the message? Do you know what the answer to that is? The answer is .... it depends upon the intensity of application of the language of the subconscious mind — and that's emotion. Repetition is important — the more often you do it, the faster the habit gets into the subconscious mind.

Language of the Subconscious Mind

The language we use is in fact another "P" — Passion, or emotion. The last exercise you did was with emotion. Eeeeemotion: energy and motion. You energise memory in the subconscious mind with how much emotion you conjure up, recall, bring back the feelings. The strength of your feelings influences how many times you need to do it. With sufficient emotion on a particular action you can indelibly print it on the subconscious mind by doing it only once.

Remember my own example of not being able to draw? I can't draw, I'll never draw again? When I was out there in front of the class, mortified, so embarrassed, so emotional.

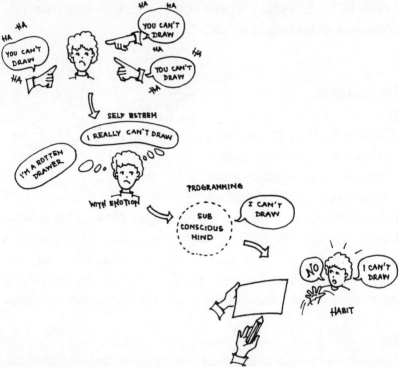

My teacher, my friends, everyone thinking I can't draw; so then I told myself. I was so embarrassed that the strength of the emotion on just that one occasion was enough for the rest of my life. I told myself: "Hey, I can't draw".

Another example: what about the early morning departure for a holiday which you've been looking forward to. You programmed your mind with emotional enjoyment to wake up early (before your alarm went off). So with enough emotion you'll only need to do it once!

The intensity of the emotion is what we're going to concentrate on right now.

Examples of Emotion

GOLD MEDAL.

Emotion for me is a number of things. Let me give you a few examples, because we're going to work a little bit with emotion. I'm actually quite an emotional person. For instance when I see an Australian sports person on television, winning a gold medal and the national anthem is played, I get such a feeling of pride for that person and for Australia that tears well in my eyes. I don't try to do it, it just happens. It's there, so it's emotional.

Another thing that's very emotional for me is watching certain movies. I can even watch a movie that I've seen before and when I see that same emotional scene again I get tears in my eyes, even though I've seen it before. A quick example is "Anne of Green Gables". My children have played that movie over and over again, but every time it comes to two or three of those scenes, I get tears in my eyes and the kids are looking up to see if Dad is crying yet!

I've now found a quick way of using that emotion: I just do everything in reverse and I can tell you about that later. I actually tried for six weeks — remember that word "try" (it implies failure) — I tried for six weeks when I was in United States, at the Insight IV course, to rid myself of this feeling of emotion. Impossible! You can't get rid of it! So what I've done now is use it to my advantage and I can show you how I've done that. (It's on page 199, so just read it when you come across it).

Now a good emotion for me was when Lara and Ian were born. After seeing both of them being born, and then just holding them in my arms I had a fantastic feeling inside of me, which I can recall quite vividly.

HOLDING A BABY

Another emotion I use quite often is involved with my time in the army. When I was in Vietnam I was in charge of the Engineer Troop which were doing a lot of booby trap work and tunnelling work (and we in fact were the first Australians, first out of the allies, who actually went down tunnels and searched them out). It was quite a challenging job; we got a lot of information out of there, and a lot of equipment. These tunnels are pretty hairy you know, every 10 feet they change in direction. You've got a torch light on your head, you've got a bayonet in one hand and a pistol in the other — you're a pretty good target as you go

around the corner of a tunnel. Some of them are so small

that you can't turn around to come out; you've got to go on and on until you come to a bigger room or a bigger area so you can turn around. Anyway I was the commander of 3 Field Troop, which was a group of engineers that searched out ¾ mile of tunnel (it's been shown on TV — *Page 1* by Chris Masters and written up in books — I've also written my own book about it called *No Need for Heroes*).

I'm very proud of the performance of the troop. Two days before I left Vietnam to come home I can remember being out in the field and my boss spoke to me on the radio and said: "Congratulations, you've just been awarded the Military Cross". I thought, "Wow! Great, this is terrific! Not only do I recognise that we did a good job but someone else recognises it as well" and I really felt good. I felt good about myself and I can bring back those feelings.

I know all of us have these feelings; all of us have felt good at some time. We need to recall the good emotion, not the bad. The good emotion is the one we're going to be putting into our Peaceful Place all the time. We want to have that good emotion there all the time, that's the one we're going to work with. This good, positive emotion can be

LOOK I CAN RIDE A BIKE!

something like: "Well done" when you just came 1st or 2nd or 3rd or 4th or 5th in a sporting event in which you have competed; or if someone puts their arm around your shoulder and says "great work" for a job you have completed, or an act of kindness; or you've just ridden a two-wheeler bike for the first time ever (and stayed on). You could have just done well in an exam and someone congratulates you. Or it could be a good feeling you had on your birthday and you can remember being hugged by someone; it may have been your wedding day; it may have been a child — yours or someone else's — saying "I love you". There are times and situations in your life about which you have felt good, and you can get in touch with that emotion.

BIRTHDAY

Emotion is the language of the subconscious mind. It is probably the single most important aspect of programming your subconscious mind. Remember what I said about the limbic system, that little "mini brain" that controls emotion. Emotion is linked to memory — that's what the scientists have told us — and that emotion is now known as the language of the subconscious mind. It's not pictures, it's not words, but it is emotion which is the language of the subconscious mind. That's why we use it, and that's why it is so important.

So there are four laws of the subconscious mind:

✦ Positive
✦ Present tense
✦ Personal
✦ Persistence

which, when used together with the language of the subconscious mind, that is:

✦   Positive Emotion (or Passion)

is extremely Powerful.

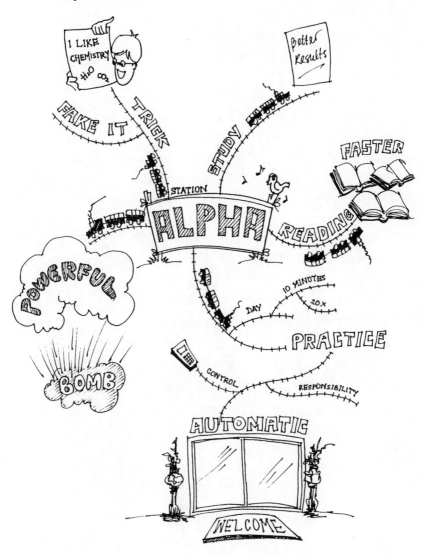

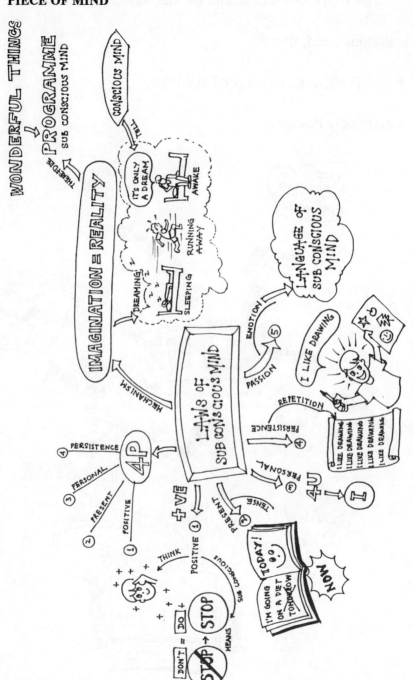

144

The subconscious mind does not know the difference between imagination and reality.

How fantastic — we can use imagination to achieve!

PREVIEW OF CHAPTER 9

9

YOUR EMOTIONAL ANCHOR

What is an Anchor?

The idea of having an "Anchor" is so that you can quickly and easily use it to your advantage. Anchors can be made and used for a variety of things. I will give you my personal example of an "Emotional Anchor", which I was taught on Insight IV. I use three fingers on my right hand (in this order): the ring finger, the middle finger and the forefinger, touching my right thigh.

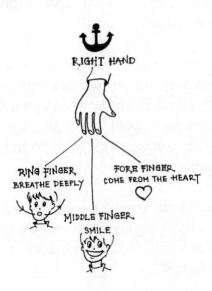

RIGHT HAND

RING FINGER
BREATHE DEEPLY

FORE FINGER
COME FROM THE HEART

MIDDLE FINGER
SMILE

The ring finger means (automatically) to me to breathe deeply; the middle finger means (automatically) to me to smile; the forefinger means (automatically) to me to "come from the heart". Then I deliberately take one pace forward and step into a "circle of excellence". I am now ready to talk and address a group or a seminar. It is a fantastic tool that takes just two seconds. My subconscious knows and recognises it because with emotion I have made it a habit.

In the same way, you can develop an Emotional Anchor which can be used to help you indelibly imprint on your subconscious mind any goal that you wish to achieve. The advantage of imprinting your goal into your subconscious mind, using emotion, is that it will happen faster; your subconscious mind will "get the message of the goal indelibly imprinted", faster. So what? Once you have the goal in your subconscious mind it then sets about directing you to achieve that goal. That's mind power! I hope that takes the mystery out of "mind power". It's a normal, natural process that we can use to achieve more!

An Emotional Anchor is used every time you wish to achieve a goal. It's a quick way of bringing back that physical feeling experienced with emotion which, when applied at the same time as programming a goal, or something you wish to achieve, helps your subconscious mind to indelibly get the "print" of the goal.

I'm sure I can hear some people saying: "Wow! You mean in a few seconds, by applying my Emotional Anchor, I'm using the language of the subconscious mind to program what I want to achieve faster?"

Yes, that's exactly what I mean!

To build the Anchor you will complete a process whereby you enhance emotion. You need to be able to tap into good positive emotion and this is how you'll do it. The process involves your Peaceful Place and preferably you'll be listening to my tape *A Peaceful Place No. 2 (Guided Imagery)*, side 2, (which uses the beautiful *Infinite Joy* music by Ken Davis with 56 beats to the minute) and you will think back to pleasant events in your life. First you'll go back just a little, in other words the last year or so, until you come to a situation that was good for you, really good. You felt good about what happened, and you felt good about yourself. It can be anything or anywhere, at work or at play. You will relive what the scene was and in your mind you will get in touch 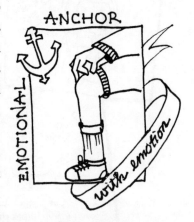 with the physical feeling that you experienced. Then you will go back a little bit more, up to say half a lifetime ago, in your mind, (you're in total control) until you find another good, positive experience. Then you will go back to let's say childhood and you will relive in your mind another one. Then you come forward in time in your mind, and as you do so you bring into your Peaceful Place one of those three scenes. Whatever scene or experience comes first is the strongest — it's the first one that comes up that will probably be the most important.

So you relive that good positive experience in your Peaceful

Place and you get in touch with the physical feeling. Let's dwell on the feeling for a moment. What are some of the feelings that you feel when you experience emotion? How do you feel the physical feeling in your body? What is it? How does it manifest in your body? What does it do to your body?

It can make you cry, make you laugh, it can make a warm feeling come right through, and in fact sometimes that warmth is a glow in your face; the feeling of lightness, like there's so much joy that you feel like floating. That physical feeling is important to bring back into your Peaceful Place every time.

Now when you relive this physical feeling, you're going to give yourself what is called an "Anchor" — your Emotional Anchor. That Emotional Anchor could be a word, which could be anything you like; or it could a touch to yourself. Take time now to choose what movement you want to use for your Anchor.

Examples of an Anchor are:

✦   Pressing with your middle finger, or say forefinger on your thigh

✦   Your finger touching your heart, lips or ear

✦   Closing your hand to make a fist

✦   Hugging yourself

✦   Clasping your hands together

✦   Or anything else that feels right for you as a "reminder"

✦   A word, for example "deep" or "feelings" or your own name spelt backwards.

So to build your Anchor, first decide on what you are going to use and apply each time you relive and experience the good positive emotional event. It is important to use the same sign every time you do it. If for some reason you do not recapture the physical feeling when you've thought of a good positive event, then know that that's OK. Apply that Anchor when you are going over the good events and reliving the experience inside your mind, because you know or imagined that you felt good at that time.

HUGGING

For some of you, recapturing feeling or emotion is difficult – many of you in life (like me) have been taught that it is not wise to show or display emotions. This means that emotions are suppressed and do not rise easily

— it's the way the subconscious mind has been trained. A way forward (if this is true for you) is to make all that OK — relive the positive event and imagine that you are feeling good. Gradually you will find emotions will come back to you. My advice is to do this exercise several times.

When the Anchor is established and you are ready to use it when setting a goal, all you do is to give yourself your sign (that is, the touch, the word, etc.) and your subconscious mind knows that it's being programmed with **extra** emotion. For those brief seconds you feel the elation, the excitement, the physical feeling of all the events that went into programming your Anchor.

Now you will program or build your Emotional Anchor. You will bring up a scene of a time when you know you felt good. Recall the environment, whatever was said — the words that were used, whatever the situation was, you'll bring it all in. Remember, if you didn't have an actual physical feeling in your body on that occasion, then that's okay, still bring back a scene when you know you felt good.

Building Your Emotional Anchor

Use my tape *A Peaceful Place No.2 (Guided Imagery)* side 2. If you don't have my tape, you can make your own over baroque music (at 56 to 64 beats per minute) using the words below.

This side of the tape will take you through the steps to

establish an Emotional Anchor — be it a word of your choosing or a sign that you give yourself, such as a touch of a finger on your thigh or on your heart — the Anchor is for a "trigger" or "reminder" of the physical feeling experienced when you recalled a good positive emotion. Take time now to choose what movement you want to use for your Anchor. To develop the Anchor you use it at the peak of the good physical feeling. It is essential that you can attain your Peaceful Place as shown on side 1 of this tape before proceeding with side 2. The following is a transcript from my tape:

Get into a comfortable position, ... take a deep breath, and as you breathe out.....let go all the stresses and tensions that are around you ... just let them all go .... Now breathe in again and gently close your eyes .... And once again, in your mind, find your magical Peaceful Place, the calming scene that you built yourself, inside your mind ... know that you're there ... use all your senses ... seeing ... listening, hearing ... and feeling, touching and smelling ... know that you're really there .... Now, in that Peaceful Place, you go on a journey .... you know that at all times you and you alone are in total control ...... the journey is back in time in your life, just a little bit ... and as you go back in your life, you seek a situation, an event that comes to you readily, comes to you easily, which was really good for you. You really felt good there ... So you describe that to yourself using all your senses .... bring it in now ... were there people there? or were you by yourself? What could you hear? ... What's being said? ... And now, how do you feel?..... What is that physical feeling in your body, that you feel, when you felt oh, so good? ... Recognise that and as you do, apply your Anchor at the height of feeling so good ... Use your special sign — is it a touch

— *or is it a word ... And now, you move back a little bit more in time in your life..... and maybe you move back to a situation which is half a lifetime ago .... So you find another time, and another place, and another event when you really felt good ... you really felt good about yourself ... and what do you see? ... or what do you hear? ... or what is it that you feel around you? Bring all that in ... and now, in bringing that in, get in touch with that feeling that is through your body ... that really good feeling in your body ... and as you now get in touch with that feeling you give yourself that same Anchor....that same word ..or that same touch..... now, you go back a little bit more in your life ... you may even go right back as far as childhood, and when you do, you come to an event when you felt so fantastic..... something really good, ...maybe in your childhood ..... And you bring in the scene, and you bring in the sounds ...... you picture and see in your mind exactly what is happening .... Let that happen ... Get in touch with it ... is somebody putting their arm around you? .... Is somebody saying "Well done!"? ..... Is somebody just giving you a hug? ..... Whatever it is, you bring that feeling forward, that feeling that is so powerful inside of you ... that physical feeling, of feeling really good inside your body.....and as you do, you give yourself that same Anchor ... that same word or touch .... You now move slowly back to your Peaceful Place, and so once again in your mind ... see and feel and hear that Peaceful Place ..... And you've just got in contact with three emotional times, and the first one that comes to you now is the most powerful. And so as that most powerful emotion comes to you in your Peaceful Place, you relive once again that event. Whatever that event is, bring it in ... and see it, and feel it, and hear it, and bring that in to you .... Now, you give yourself your anchor .... Your anchor now can be used to get in touch with that feeling of feeling good that's inside you ....*

you can use it as an automatic action .... So recognise that feeling, and NOW ... give yourself that anchor.....Yes you can smile using your anchor .... And so you know that your anchor brings back for you that emotional physical feeling into your Peaceful Place .... Or for you it may bring back the description of the event where you felt oh so good, and that's fine. ... that's fine ..... So now on the count of five you will open your eyes, knowing that you will have that anchor, which will bring that great feeling back into your Peaceful Place. ONE — your fingers and toes start to tingle a little bit, feeling the blood circulating. TWO — you move your fingers and toes a little bit, and THREE, you just stretch a bit. FOUR, you roll your neck around. FIVE — eyes open, wide awake, feeling relaxed well healthy and invigorated knowing your anchor will bring back that wonderful feeling that you've experienced.

Some of you may have actually lost the feeling of your body during that exercise, which means that you're probably going well past Alpha down into Theta. However, as I said before, your mind is still totally alert, and you know exactly what you're doing and you are directing it. (The way to tell the difference between Alpha and Theta is that with Theta you lose the feeling in your body). Nevertheless, you're working in Alpha and you'll be doing this in 30 second bursts. (It takes at least 10 to 15 minutes for those who practise to get into the Theta state — this is the real meditative state).

Exercise

The reason for this exercise is to involve our other learning

modes. I would like you to write down in the space provided, the event that you actually brought back into your Peaceful Place — that one event that's most important to you. Put in all the emotion as you write about it. Right now, I hope you are feeling warm, glowing and great about yourself. The more you tell yourself about good events and good things that happen the better it is. This is how you can start building on self esteem. Great leaders work this way. There's something good about everybody, just remember that. Especially with raising children, take one thing, be it sports, something academic, something loving about their nature, and build on that. Tell them how great they are, and they will know and recognise that they are good at that, and it will help to build their self esteem. Continually reinforce the positive, even if it is only one good thing, and then there is a spill over effect to other areas. It's one of the most positive things that we can do for ourselves, or our children.

....

....

....

....

....

....

....

....

....

Letting Go Thoughts

During the Emotional Anchor process you may have

experienced invasion into your mind of many thoughts; thoughts that you did not invite in and maybe that you could have done without. Working with emotion generally does that. Did lots of thoughts come in and then go out? Or did lots of thoughts come in and hang around? Did any of these thoughts present what you might think of as a "problem"? In other words you couldn't get rid of them? Remember, a way to let them go is by putting thoughts on an escalator or on a plane, or in one ear and out the other and just letting them go. So take control — practise letting them go and they will go.

Using Thoughts to your Advantage

Some thoughts are bad thoughts — you can take control of these too. I'd like to tell you a little bit about bad thoughts and good thoughts. You can in fact gain benefit from both bad thoughts and good thoughts. How can that be you ask? If for example the thought comes into your mind that you could really just about strangle somebody, how can you use that to your advantage? What you can do is to say "no" to that bad thought. That's all! Once again take control. So as this bad thought comes flowing into you, what you have the choice of doing is saying "no" to it. What happens when you say "no" to a bad thought? It can go away, or you can send it away. That's one thing that can happen; but in addition, by you taking the good positive action of saying "no" to the bad thought, your self esteem is raised. Your self talk is positive, so that effects your self esteem; you feel better about yourself by saying "no" to the bad thought. Remember, the next step in the "esteem process"? Your self esteem gradually becomes your self image, and that's what gets into the subconscious mind where you feel good about yourself. So you can have the bad thought and say "no" to it and by doing so, can turn it into a good feeling. Good thoughts of course are already good and positive, so when they come in they go into your self image. Remember with bad thoughts you **can** end up with a positive experience, and as good thoughts are already good, we can say: all thoughts can have a positive experience. With bad thoughts, only if you accept them are they bad thoughts, but if you can reject them, if you can say "no" to them, then you can change the feeling inside you to a good feeling. So use every good thought and every bad thought to increase your own self image and feel better about yourself. Try it, you'll be amazed at the positive effects.

Remember what I've said about thoughts. You're not responsible for all your thoughts. So once again, take control, let them go and never give the thought any power. You have the power and so that's just one more "mystery of mind power" banished — it's all gone — **you** have the power. Keep building up your own self image every moment you can, it's great for your subconscious mind!

Grief and Emotion

Some of you may get stuck with the emotion exercise, because of an event involving the loss of someone close to you. If for example the good emotion you are tapping into is the loving, caring warmth of your mother, but your mother is no longer alive and you are unable to tap into just the good-

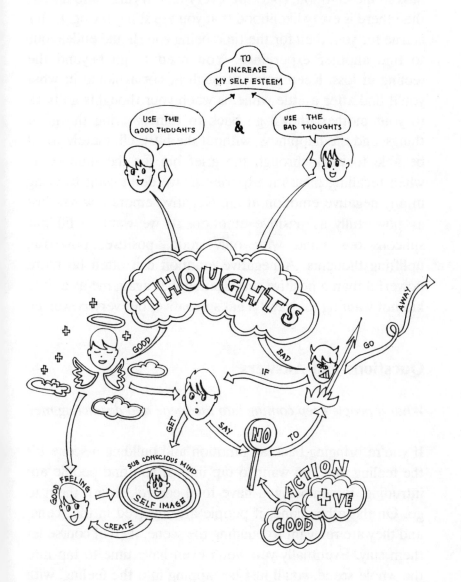

ness in the emotion, (because every time it turns into a loss) then there is every likelihood that you are still grieving. If this is true for you, then for the time being you should endeavour to find another experience. You need to go beyond the feeling of loss. Keep going through it, not avoiding it; what you'll find after a little while, is when your thoughts go back to your mother, they'll go back to remembering the good things, and the happiness, without the hurt. Ultimately you'll be able to work through the grief but for the time being when recalling pleasant experiences we don't want to bring in any negative emotion at all. Negative emotion works just as powerfully as positive emotion, so we want to fill our subconscious mind with only good, positive, powerful, uplifting thoughts. A negative emotion can often be more powerful than a positive one. Remember again me as a little kid not wanting to draw? That's negative, but very powerful.

Questions and Answers

What if people keep coming into the scene and distracting me?

If you're bringing back an emotion and building a scene it's the feeling that you want to tap into. If you find people are intruding, remember you have total control, so tell them to go. On the other hand, if people are involved in the scene, and they are relevant to building the scene, then of course let them stay. Eventually you won't even have time to tap into the whole scene, you'll just be tapping into the feeling, with your Emotional Anchor, and it will only take a second or two.

What if we're listening to a good news stations — at some stage they're bound to come through with some bad news. How do I handle the bad news?

Yes, what you're saying is so true and bad news can be the source of negative thoughts. If you're expecting it, for example at "News Time", you could turn it off. There will always bad news. A way of handling the bad news, to the best of your ability, is to treat it as a thought you don't want, ie. just let it go. Another thought is to just treat the news as information, ie. don't put on it the connotation of good news or bad news. Of course you can always control the TV and radio program that you tune into.

As far as newspapers are concerned, you can choose what to read or what NOT to read — you're the boss. I'd suggest to you to be very discerning.

How about negative people, any tips on how to handle them?

When you come in contact with negative people, one good thing to do is just send out good thought waves, send out love for instance (silently in your mind). Remember, whatever you give out, you get back. So if you want love or good relationships and good thoughts then send out love or good relationships or good thoughts. Many people often use negative language and that's fine; some may not know the importance of being more constructive. You just do your own thing, being positive and constructive.

I find it hard to get an emotion or a feeling — any suggestions?

Go to your Peaceful Place and think of good events in your life. If necessary go to a time when you were a child and there was a special event like receiving a present — birthdays, Christmas, parties, picnics, etc. Then listen to the tape *A Peaceful Place No. 2 (Guided Imagery)*, side two once again (you can't do it too often). You will find that recalling the good event, with you knowing you felt good at that time will be sufficient to start the cycle of emotion and feelings to take effect. You will probably also find that emotions will "loosen up" and come to the surface. This process is to be encouraged.

My negative emotion invades me in my Peaceful Place — what can I do about it?

Negative emotion can often tend to dominate our thought processes, acting like a protection mechanism, eg. ".... this is what happened before ...." Treat the negative emotion just like an invading thought. You have power over it (the thought) so just let it go — in one ear and out the other, or attach it to a never ending escalator, or put it in a plane flying overhead. You must actually do this in your mind over and over again until it goes.

I did not get any physical feeling in my body when I formed my Emotional Anchor — how does this effect me using it?

Many of us have been taught not to show our emotions —

"sign of weakness", "don't cry", etc., and our bodies have learned to suppress the resultant physical feelings. With practice in recalling pleasant emotional events [using the tape: *A Peaceful Place No. 2 (Guided Imagery)* is a great way] we can get in touch not only with more positive events, but the physical feeling as well. The goal process is just as powerful, even when you do not recognise the physical feeling — apply your Emotional Anchor and at the same time recall quickly the good positive event, and how you felt at that time. This of course adds to the good feeling of seeing yourself succeed in your goal. By doing this there is a resultant emotion, which you may not at first recognise, but this helps to indelibly imprint the success of your goal in your subconscious mind.

REVIEW OF CHAPTER 9

*We have at least
50,000 thoughts a day.*

*Make sure this
"self talk"
is positive ....
because....
guess who's listening?*

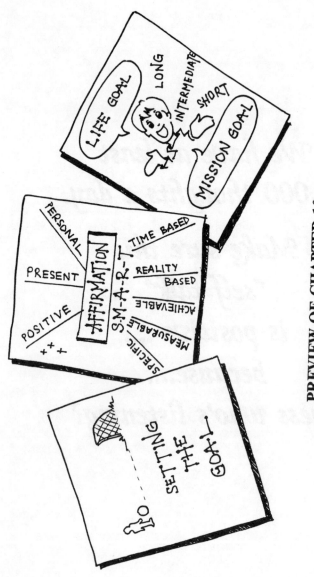

PREVIEW OF CHAPTER 10

10

SETTING THE GOAL

The fastest way of achieving a change of direction, or to make a change of any kind in your life, is to program your subconscious mind with the end result. All meaningful and lasting change commences on the inside (of you) and works its way out. You may not immediately be able to change your circumstances, but you can certainly ultimately change your life by changing your attitudes — make the most of today. Once you succeed in having clear, concise, vividly expressed goals in your subconscious mind, your own creativity starts to work to achieve the desired goal (or habit change). Indeed you may create sub goals which in fact lead to the major goal, so that the "reality" inside of you commences to show itself "outside of you". The achievement of this is the subject of the next two chapters of this book.

The two main parts of goal setting are (once you know the new direction or change) to:

1.   State the goal in concise, positive, present tense and personal language (the written goal is sometimes known as an affirmation).

2.   Ensure that the stated goal is "SMART":

- S   – Specific
- M   – Measurable
- A   – Achievable
- R   – Reality based
- T   – Time based

A very important aspect of goal setting is that they must be balanced. In other words they support your total life. To achieve this, areas of life that need to be considered are:

✦   Marriage and Family Goals

✦   Sport and Health Goals

✦   Success and Job Goals

✦   Education and Further Education Goals

✦   Social and Leisure Goals

✦   Personal Development and Spiritual Goals.

Collective consideration of the above goals can lead to a "life" goal or "mission" goal.

Another point is the setting of: —

—	3 to 5 year goals :	→ Long Term Goals
—	1 year goals :	→ Intermediate Goals
—	1 Day/Week/Month Goals :	→ Short term goals

It's the short term goals that lead to your "next action" steps.

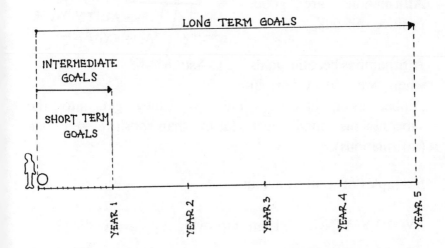

An old Chinese proverb states: "The Journey of 1,000 miles starts with a single step." It is also important to remember that your long term goals are not "set in concrete", they can be adjusted as you gain additional information.

You can use your own subconscious mind to tell you what your goals may be or what you could and should take into account when setting your goal — you get the help of your own subconscious mind.

Affirmations

Remember that the affirmations you use towards achieving your goals are Positive, Present tense and Personal statements. These are the laws of the subconscious mind. Recognise them? Affirmations are good, positive self talk.

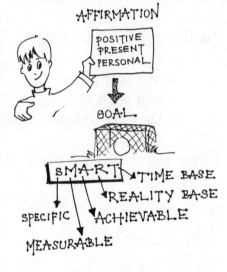

Affirmations become goals when we do them in Alpha, using emotion. This way they get into the subconscious mind much faster than positive self talk (affirmations).

Examples of what to avoid:

AVOID SAYING: "I am improving my slow reading"

INSTEAD, SAY: "I am reading faster every day."

Remember the "don't" in "Don't think of a rainbow"? – keep it positive – what **DO** you want? Remember what the subconscious thought of tomorrow? It never comes! It only operates in the present tense. Never use statements that include "maybe" or "some day". Time constraints must be handled with care for you could, by having an aim set too far into the future, prevent the possibility of earlier accomplishment of the aim. On the other hand, you could introduce an element of procrastination by doing things at the last minute (like mowing the lawn or weeding the garden).

For example —

NOT: "I will work in a better, new job in 12 months time",

RATHER: "I have a fantastic, satisfying job".

This way you allow your subconscious mind to work at helping you find a great job immediately. You could introduce a time element such as:

"I have a fantastic, satisfying new job by at least ....", (you state the date, making it twelve months in advance and adding "at least" — thus allowing the possibility of earlier accomplishment). You could also introduce a salary element so that your goal is more specific, and indeed the industry you wish to work in.

"I am a clerk in the Sydney Stock Exchange on an annual salary of $30,000 by ...." (insert the date).

By now you have seen how you use "personal" language. You never have an affirmation which is to have a change in another person. You control you. It is **your** self image you are changing. In all affirmations, except team ones, you'll be safe if you start yours with "I".

Within the words of the statement it's a great idea if you use "exciting" and "doing" words, for instance: "happy", "loving", "enjoying", "easy, "firm". Never use comparisons like "as good as" or "better than" – you work on the best you can be.

The S-M-A-R-T Test

It's worth repeating, always check to see if your affirmation is:

S	–	Specific
M	–	Measurable
A	–	Achievable
R	–	Reality based
T	–	Time based.

The affirmation should be as short and as concise as possible – only one goal in one affirmation.

Your goal must be "believable" by you. This is one of the reasons that goals are generally kept close to your chest; you don't need the hindrance of your friends or family not supporting you, or not believing in your ability to achieve a goal. You certainly can stretch yourself in your goal, but you must base it on your own reality. If it's believable by you, then it's achievable.

I've already spoken about time. Sometimes you need to put a time statement in, sometimes not. To achieve a goal within a time structure it's most appropriate to say: "I easily achieve 90% in my final school exams in .... (insert date)"

I WEIGHT 61 KILOGRAMS BY MAY 1992

Some example affirmations that may help you are:

I weigh 61 kilograms by .... (insert date)

I release 1 kilogram per week until I weigh ....

I enjoy the daily exercises at my gymnasium

I pay cash for a new car by ....

I add a new bedroom to my house by ....

I easily keep my filing up to date

I enjoy making appointments by telephone

I enjoy being organised

I am fair in all my dealings

I conduct 5 successful meetings each week

I exude warmth and happiness

I read at least one book each week

I go on an overseas trip by ....

I pay my bills on time

I spend four effective hours with my children each week

I easily triple my reading speed with full comprehension

I enjoyably triple my learning speed using accelerated learning techniques.

Write Down Your Goal

You are reading this book for a purpose. You could use that purpose and formulate it into a goal commencing with an affirmative statement. You could choose another goal — any goal you wish. Your goal may be relaxation and releasing stress: "I enjoy easily relaxing at will" is a good one. If you have two goals then choose, for the moment, only one and you will work with that one for the remainder of this book. Whatever it is, I now want you to write it down in the space below.

Do you know why I am asking you to write it down? Well, firstly, if you make goals, then you are amongst about 4% of people in the world — yes, only about 4% of people work with goals. The percentage of those that write them down is even less (don't ask me to verify these figures, but I've heard it in seminars time after time — it's probably a guesstimate). People don't write down goals because they don't realise the importance of doing so.

ONLY 4% of people IN THE WORLD WORK WITH GOALS

Secondly, and more importantly, because by writing down goals it is making a commitment to yourself. The minute you write something down you are making a commitment, and a lot of people do not like to commit to anything.

Exercise

So go for it, write down your goal:

....

176

....

....

Now, try to step outside yourself and objectively analyse what you have written down. Could it be more personal or more positive? Perhaps you could use a stronger descriptive word, for example: "I am doing fantastically well", instead of "I am doing well". Make sure it's all in the present tense. Now check it out to see if it's SMART.

Now is the time to check out if the wording of your goal is correct. You could ask someone whom you know and trust, or you could go to your Peaceful Place, bring in your goal and ask yourself if it's right. Take about five minutes and then modify it if that's what comes up for you. So now write down any modification to your affirmation or goal statement.

....

....

....

....

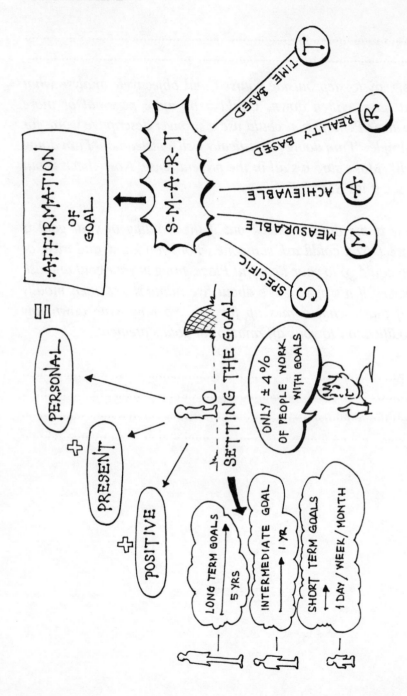

REVIEW OF CHAPTER 10

*Affirmations are good, positive statements that can become goals when you do them deliberately —
in Alpha
with emotion*

PREVIEW OF CHAPTER 11

11

IMAGING THE SUCCESS OF YOUR GOAL

The Importance of Imaging

Remember I said to you that the subconscious mind doesn't know the difference ...... can you finish it? ...... between reality and imagination. That is probably one of the most powerful statements in this book. The subconscious mind does not have a mechanism for discerning between imagination and reality. Now we can put that to use and here's how.

You now start to work with your goal, by using imagery (some people prefer to use the word "visualisation"). You will imagine what it is like, what happens when you have the success of achieving your goal. Put it into an image form, or a feeling form, or a hearing form. Sometimes it might be someone else speaking to you about achieving your goal, especially if you're an auditory person. For visual people, you're going to be able to see the scene — this is very powerful.

I'll give you a quick example. My son Andrew, when he was 24 years old, had to fly across to Perth to give a presentation.

He'd given presentations before but hadn't done one like this for his company (he was then the sales manager for a computer software company). He was called on to address customers and potential customers about their software and this was not his normal role, but this time he had to do it — it was a corporate decision and he only had three days notice. He visualised and saw himself during those three days, 50 times a day, giving that presentation. He physically went into his Peaceful Place and saw, felt and heard his presentation.

He went through the setting of the room and saw himself talking to a room full of clients. He did it about 50 times, on each of these three days before his talk. He saw it so vividly; he imagined that he saw people that he knew were going to be there; he saw the support staff he had. He saw people stand up and clap when it was over; he saw people jump up and he saw half a dozen people put their arms around his shoulders and say "Well done Andrew, good job". So he did this 50 times each day in his mind for three days and of course the 50 times only takes about 15 seconds each time.

When he actually went to do the presentation, it was as though his subconscious mind had done it already, many times before, so he physically gave the presentation brilliantly! Not only brilliantly, but it was uncannily accurate; three or four people sprang out of their chairs and said "Well done". He got half a dozen slaps across the shoulder in the next break and in fact people were saying "Well done Andrew, good job". It was almost exactly the way he'd programmed it in his mind. So just 150 times it took him, 20 minutes a day for those three days and he prepared himself for what he needed to do.

Now Andrew (before this talk) was not in his comfort zone giving this sort of presentation. In fact there were quite a series of doubts raised in his mind as to his own abilities. How did he overcome this? Remember once again that the subconscious mind does not know the difference between imagination and reality. By placing his goal into his subconscious mind, imaging the end result and feeling really good about his performance, he created the reality inside his subconscious mind. In other words he expanded his comfort zone inside his subconscious mind to be familiar with presenting to his clients. Inside his own subconscious mind he overcame any doubts as to his abilities, because he saw the end result. When he actually gave the presentation his subconscious mind was familiar, his self image was indelibly imprinted with a great performance and that's what he gave. Great stuff! So the habit change started on the inside first and then it worked its way out!

You too will be doing this: creating new comfort zones inside your subconscious mind and using affirmations and imagery

183

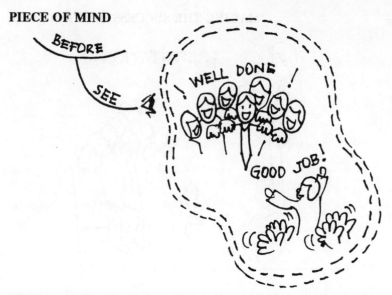

(which utilises the fact that the subconscious mind has no mechanism for discerning between imagination and reality) – you will overcome fears and doubts and blocks. "Nothing happens unless first a dream. What a man dares to dream, he becomes".

There is one more extremely important tool to use in programming the subconscious mind, and that is the language – emotion reinforced with your Emotional Anchor. In the next chapter **"Putting it all Together"** you will learn how to effectively use emotions so that you can achieve your goals faster. Enough emotion can indelibly etch the subconscious very quickly (once again, the example of me as a kid hating drawing).

Self Confidence – Imagery

Some of you may have a self-confidence goal: to be more self-confident. What you need to do is to find a situation whereby you can see yourself being confident. In other words how would your behaviour be if you were confident. It's so important that I'll remind you again: the subconscious mind doesn't know the difference between reality and imagination. Whether or not you have been in the situation you're describing to yourself before and perhaps never even behaved in this confident manner, doesn't matter two hoots. What is important is that you see yourself doing precisely what you want, in precisely the way in which you want to behave. A good clue sometimes is to see someone else who is extremely confident in the same situation you have described to yourself.

What you do is bring that person in to your Peaceful Place, see them in the same situation, then you step into their shoes, whilst they leave your Peaceful Place, so that you pick up that same feeling of confidence. Imagine how you would

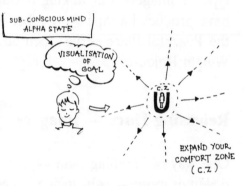

apply this to making successful telephone calls for your business. It's important to visualise people wanting the information you have to impart. Go the extra step — visualise having successful meetings with them. Visualise how your calls and meetings add to the success of your business.

Weight Release — Imagery

For a weight release goal you picture a number of things. You see yourself at the weight you want to be. You physically see the clothes that you fit into and what you look like. If it's a particular weight that you want to be, let's say its 8½ stone — or 53 kilos — you picture yourself getting onto the scales, looking down, and hey! the scales are on 8½ stone, (or 53 kilos) — exactly what you want to be! You picture yourself in front of a mirror, and when you look into that mirror you see yourself the shape that you want to be. There are many more things with weight, like leaving a bit of food on the side of your plate, chewing thoroughly, not serving yourself as much, etc, etc. That's the type of imagery I'm talking about. I have produced a tape — number 8 in the Peaceful Place series, focused on Weight Release.

WEIGHT

Releasing Hurt — Imagery

One way of handling pain — and there are probably half a dozen or more — is by giving it a colour. Actually it's not the pain you release but the hurt that is in the pain. The pain is actually a signal that something is out of "alignment" in the body. You can work at releasing the hurt, but keep the signal (the pain) until your body is "re-aligned". Let's say you see the pain as the colour red. Firstly you intensify the hurt concentrated on it, increase it in your mind (incidentally that means you're controlling it when you can increase it — if you can increase it, then you can decrease it). Now bring the colour red into the hurt, see (or feel) the hurt as red. Then select your favourite colour or select a colour that means something to you which indicates feeling good. It might be green, it might be blue, but whatever it is you see the red going away and at the same time see the blue (or whatever colour you've selected) filling it up and taking its place. See all the red going and the new colour replacing it. If you want to see it going away in a particular direction then I'd suggest you make it go out through the top of your head. There it goes.

Now bring in the other colour in the same way. That's the beginning of handling or taking control of the hurt. For Meditation or Healing you direct your mind in the Theta state — that is the directed healing state — the state just above sleep. There are many meditation tapes available for assistance in this subject area. Mine are listed in the back of this book, starting on page 230.

Quit Smoking — Imagery

Quitting smoking is a good one but quite a difficult one for me because I've never smoked. There are two ways that one can go about this — either cold turkey or just a little bit at a time. I suggest that you do it

a little bit at a time. So if you smoke 20 cigarettes a day then you need to come down to 15 and then to 10 and then to 5 and then to 1 and then to none. Remember, one thing not to say is: "I don't smoke", because what does that mean to your subconscious mind? It means: "I smoke — give me a cigarette". What you could picture is a scene of you having a cigarette, but feeling ill and vomiting because the cigarette tastes like .... (the worst thing you can think of). Another way is to picture a scene where you normally have a cigarette and in that scene see yourself not having that cigarette. You see yourself congratulating yourself and saying "Well done" to yourself every time you don't have a cigarette. If you start hankering after a cigarette, then remind yourself what it tastes like. A good goal is "I have healthy lungs and a clean breath."

Exercise

*What you need to do now is to practise imagery or visualisation. The task is to know what scenes (or imagery) are right for you to represent the success of your aim or goal. You can do this in any way that you want. Take about five minutes and get that feeling, get that scene. I suggest that you use my tape A Peaceful Place No. 1 (Instrumental), with the **Infinite Joy** music. You could of course play the baroque music tapes. You could if you wish go to your Peaceful Place inside your mind and ask yourself for the imagery.*

Questions and Answers

My goal is to build up my body and I chose an intermediate goal to help me, this being weight lifting, which I have never done. What do I do now?

Before you start physically weight lifting you bring in your goal, see yourself doing weight lifting, enjoying it, see your body developing the way you want, feel good about yourself and use your Emotional Anchor. After two weeks or so you will have an attitude of "let me at those weights" — and you'll do it.

My goal seems so distant, as I know it cannot happen for several years. What do you suggest I do?

It is important to break down your goal into what is achievable in — five years, one year and perhaps one month. The monthly goal is a stepping stone to the yearly goal, and the annual goal is a stepping stone towards the five year goal. It is best to concentrate on your monthly goal which then is not so distant and you know you are achieving.

If I want to just use the Peaceful Place for releasing stress, what do I do?

When you have got to your Peaceful Place, then relaxation and releasing stress are automatic. You really only need to keep getting to your Peaceful Place and staying there for a few seconds. If you have a particular event that causes the stress then you could treat the action of getting through that event without increasing stress, the same way as you would a goal.

I saw my Peaceful Place and got to it the first time. Now, as much as I try, I don't see it. Is it important to see it?

The short answer is — No. The thing to do is remain calm and imagine that you are seeing your Peaceful Place. Check it out in your mind. If you keep **trying** (remember that implies failure) your level of anxiety increases and it's not important to see, so just imagine that you are seeing it or checking it out.

How do I help my insomnia?

Go to your Peaceful Place whilst in bed ready to fall asleep then tell yourself that you're going to sleep whilst in your magic chair. You may need to play the tape if you feel too stressed to tell yourself the steps of the process of going into your Peaceful Place. Many people find it most beneficial to listen to the tape (especially until you are used to the process and feel confident to do it by yourself) to guide them on their way to their Peaceful Place. (I now have a tape *A Peaceful Place No. 12 — Making Sleep Easy and Useful*, which addresses the area of insomnia — see page 232).

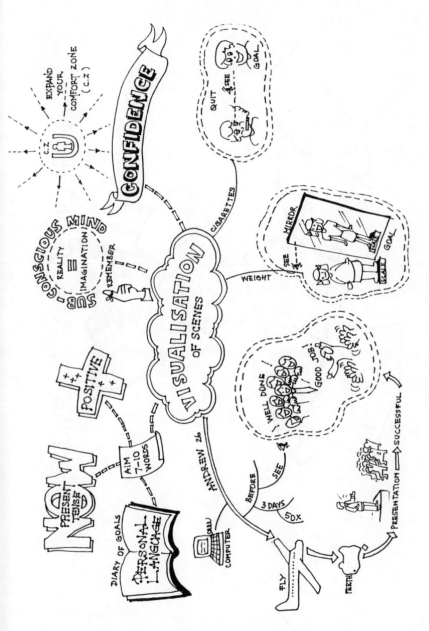

PUTTING IT ALL TOGETHER,

PREVIEW OF CHAPTER 12

12

PUTTING IT ALL TOGETHER

Sequence

You've now read everything that you need to, to move on to putting all the information together, to achieve goals faster, to overcome blocks, fears and doubts, and to achieve each goal within your extended comfort zone. The steps to do this are:

1. Comfortable position

2. Take a deep breath and close your eyes

3. Go to your Peaceful Place

4. Roll your eyes up and down

5. Bring in your goal in Positive, Present tense and Personal language

6. Sense yourself achieving your goal and feel good

7. Use your Emotional Anchor – tap into the physical feeling

8.   Count back 1 to 5 or take a deep breath.

That's it! That's as simple as it is! Now there should be no mystery to "Mind Power".

Most people describe and teach Mind Power as Affirmations (self talk) and Visualisation. For true Mind Power to be achieved you must use your subconscious effectively by doing goals and visualisation in the Alpha state using the language of the subconscious mind — **Emotion.**

Achieving Goals Faster

To reiterate: we're endeavouring to program our sub-conscious mind with a goal until it becomes the habit, or the reality. The subconscious mind then brings forward the goal into reality. How fast this happens depends upon Persistence and Emotion: How often do you do it? Can you bring forward emotion or that physical feeling? Re-program the subconscious mind with your goal, using the language of the subconscious. Remember my personal example of releasing 22 kilos with nothing happening (or so I thought) for six weeks? I did it three times a day, 20 minutes a day, for six

1. COMFORTABLE POSITION
2. DEEP BREATH & CLOSE YOUR EYES
3. PEACEFUL PLACE
4. EYES UP & DOWN
5. GOAL
6. SEE IT COMING TRUE
7. EMOTIONAL ANCHOR
8. COUNT 1 TO 5

weeks before I started losing any weight at all. You know why? Because I didn't know anything about emotion at that time. Of course a lot of people teaching "mind methods" also did not know then or understand the importance of using emotion. Emotion is the key that would start a weight release process within two weeks. Another thing: when I was doing it, I was proving it (mind power) to myself. There was no way I wanted to tell myself to go and eat less or to go on a diet or that I wanted to do exercise. If I did those things then there would have been other elements working to help release weight. What I wanted to do was to prove that this mind method worked. So if in fact you are going on a weight release program, I would suggest that you look at exercise and better eating habits right from the start. They're important, but for me it was different. I needed to prove to myself that "mind power" works. Many people who have weight release as their goal, release one kilogram in the second week!

This programming can really work fast. One excited gentleman told me that he had never won a golf tournament in his life and after learning the technique he applied it to golf. For every shot he had on the course he applied Alpha; he won the tournament and he played the best golf he'd ever played. Now some could say that's coincidence and sure, it could be coincidence. However, he had just done the course and he went out and used what he had learned and applied Alpha to every shot and he did well. It can happen quickly, very quickly.

For those who suffer from insomnia, using the Peaceful Place method of getting into Alpha (which is the first step in going to sleep) and then just dropping off to sleep in your Peaceful Place, has proven a very quick and effective method to get to sleep.

Putting it all Together

You will now program your subconscious mind with your goal in your Peaceful Place, using positive, present tense and personal language; you then imagine the goal coming true and at the same time charge it with emotion. Thus the goal is achieved in the subconscious mind first, and remember, all meaningful and lasting change takes place on the inside first, before it becomes a fact in conscious life.

Play the tape *A Peaceful Place No. 2 (Guided Imagery)* side two *Putting it all Together*. Here is a transcript of the tape.

Now, just take a deep breath, and let it all out − this is your goal coming up. Now let's take another deep breath, and at the same time close your eyes, and go to your Peaceful Place. Make this quiet Peaceful Place as real as you can. Now in that Peaceful Place, bring in your goal ... in personal, positive and present tense language ... now see yourself achieving that goal ... visualise it, imagine it coming true, and as you do so ... emotionalise it, bring in that emotion by using your Emotional Anchor ... and then count yourself back from 1 to 5, and on 5, open your eyes.

Now we'll just go a fraction faster. I'm going to say raise your eyes up, then down − because that puts you straight into Alpha. That's the signal for the subconscious mind to say: "Hey I'm in the Alpha state, I'm on the way to sleep" but then the conscious mind takes over. As I said before, if you don't like rolling up your eyes, then don't do it. This is all very individual, so just do just whatever is right for you.

Take a deep breath, and at the same time, close your eyes. Now go to your Peaceful Place ... raise your eyes up and down ... now, bring in your goal : personal, positive and present tense language. See the success of that goal, hear it and feel it ... and now emotionalise it by using your anchor.....recognise that great feeling. Now count yourself back from 1 to 5 and on 5 open your eyes.

Let's do it again and this time you can just take a deep breath without counting back from 1 to 5 before you open your eyes: .... now take a deep breath, close your eyes, go to your Peaceful Place, roll your eyes up then down, bring in your goal in personal positive and present tense language..... visualise it coming true ... see it, feel it or hear it ... now bring in that emotion, that anchor. Now take a deep breath and open your eyes.

OK, let's do it again, just a fraction faster. Take a deep breath, and let it all out − that's the idea. Now take another deep breath, and at the same time close your eyes and go to your Peaceful Place. Roll your eyes up then down ... and now in personal, positive and present tense language, bring in your goal ... now visualise it, and see it happening, and now emotionalise it with your anchor ... and now take a deep breath and open your eyes.

Now we'll do it again just using one word cues. So, take a deep breath, close your eyes, Peaceful Place, eyes up and down, goal, see it coming true, Emotional Anchor, deep breath and eyes open.

Do that once more and then you can do it a few times again later. So, deep breath, close your eyes, Peaceful Place, roll your eyes up then down, goal, visualise it coming true, Emotional Anchor, deep breath and eyes open.

I hope you enjoyed the tape and found the last three minutes of the music fruitful for doing the practice at your own rate. If you found the tape a bit too fast, (actually you were doing the whole cycle in 30 seconds) then that's OK, because you can practise at your own speed. In doing the complete cycle you were not only imagining getting your goal and emotionalising it, you were actually doing it in the relaxed Alpha state. So you also achieved relaxation. By achieving relaxation, stress goes. So now, if you're at work and you feel stress building up, go to your Peaceful Place. Ten seconds is all it takes. You relax. If you feel it build again — it only takes ten seconds to relax. Feel it build again — ten seconds you relax. It's so fast to achieve — it's for the busy person.

Gradually when you practise it more and more, you can do it with your eyes open — it's called staring! When you keep practising to release stress, all you're doing is making a neural pathway to your Peaceful Place. What's automatic in your Peaceful Place? Stress goes. So just practising getting to your Peaceful Place is really great, because you release stress, and then when you're in Alpha state you're really paying attention to whatever your goal is, with single focused concentration. Keep practising this twenty times a day,

thirty seconds at a time, that is, ten minutes a day for a month. It's then the best habit you could possibly have, and it will save you heaps of time in your busy life.

I promised (on page 140) that I would tell you how I use emotion in reverse. If emotion comes up for me in a movie, then I take advantage of it by quickly going to my Peaceful Place, bringing in a goal and then using the emotion which is still around to reinforce my goal once again (because it only takes a few seconds to do it). It's a great use for all the surplus emotion!

Exercise

Write down the eight steps to program your goals in your subconscious mind:

1. ....

2. ....

3. ....

4. ....

5. ....

6. ....

7. ....

8. ....

Play A Peaceful Place No. 1 (Instrumental), and do the above eight steps six times (do it at your leisure), using your goal. After you have completed it, pat yourself on the back and say "Well done".

Questions and Answers

After being in Alpha and opening your eyes is there any other reinforcing action that can be taken?

When I come back from one to five and open my eyes I always say "I'm relaxed, well, healthy and invigorated". I just use those four words. I use it often in my seminars and would encourage you to do something similar. In fact you create another good positive habit every time you use those words.

How do I handle exam stress?

The main way is to physically see yourself going through this test or exam inside your mind. See how well you are doing it, feel good about it, even look at the mark that you're going to obtain. Just notice all that and then emotionalise it. When you actually do the exam your subconscious mind has done it so often before that it's a habit. What has happened is that you have extended your comfort zone to include the exam. You are really utilising the fact that the subconscious mind does not know the difference between imagination and reality. If you feel uptight before an exam another thing to do is to breathe. Just take a deep breath because when you take a deep breath you're letting oxygen in and you will relax. Also remember throughout the year when you're learning the information, it helps to study in Alpha.

Does the emotion used in establishing the Emotional Anchor need to be the same type of emotion when emotionalising a goal?

The emotion that you bring back with your Emotional Anchor is actually the physical feeling of feeling good. It need not have any relationship to the goal at all. You're converting emotion to a feeling in the body; how it was originally created doesn't matter (as long as the experience was positive). What was it that I said about the subconscious mind? It does not know the difference between reality and imagination. So you're fooling the subconscious mind with the use of the emotion, by only tapping into the physical feeling, not the circumstances when you use your Emotional Anchor.

In an exam, how do I use Alpha for remembering the answer when I get stuck?

Go to your Peaceful Place and ask yourself the question. See yourself getting the answer with a tick next to it, then go on with the next question. You will find the answer suddenly comes to you whilst doing another question. (See the tape *A Peaceful Place No. 11 — Achieving in Exams and Effective Study*, page 232).

I put things down and then can't find them. Help please!

The major reason is that you didn't pay attention to where you put them, that's why you don't know where they are. Take just a fraction of a second to pay attention to where you put them. For one fraction of a second look at the spot where you are going to put something down, let's say your wallet, and pretend to yell "wallet" inside your mind. It could be "wallet" and "table" to associate the fact that your wallet is on the table. That's all, just for one fraction of a second. Now for that one fraction of a second it's like recalling your mother's maiden name. You access Alpha, for that one fraction of a second staring at the spot where you put your wallet and saying "**WALLET**", "**TABLE**"! That triggers, the memory response inside your mind. In fact you open up your filter of the Reticular Activating System. Try that — it works!

Can you get too relaxed? So relaxed that you cannot perform your tasks?

When you are very relaxed and tired, and you stay in the Alpha state for a while — guess what the next step is? That's right — Theta, and then of course Delta — deep sleep. Unless of course you stop yourself by your conscious mind directing you. As to any tasks you have, you will achieve them faster in Alpha.

I find background music distracting. What shall I do?

Turn it off — it's not an absolute essential.

Do you have to close your eyes?

No. Have you ever seen someone else, or caught yourself, staring. That's the Alpha state. Single focused concentration. You are not looking at anything when you're staring, but your mind is fixed on a subject. Small children do it often and easily — you can train yourself to do it.

I keep forgetting small things like my pen or business cards and I think I'm losing my memory. Can you use Alpha to assist?

When do you remember that you have forgotten something? Oh, as soon as you leave your house? Well, then do you say "Oh darn I've forgotten my keys!" (or whatever it might be)? When you're saying "forget" you're reinforcing "forget" in the subconscious mind. I forgot, I forgot, I forgot. Do you know it's not even the truth! The truth is you've just **remembered** your keys! If you always say, "I just remembered my keys", then what you're reinforcing in the subconscious mind is **remember**. "I just remembered my keys." So, change your self talk, that is really important. Positive language is very, very important. Remember self talk becomes self esteem and our self esteem becomes our self image and the way we actually act in life.

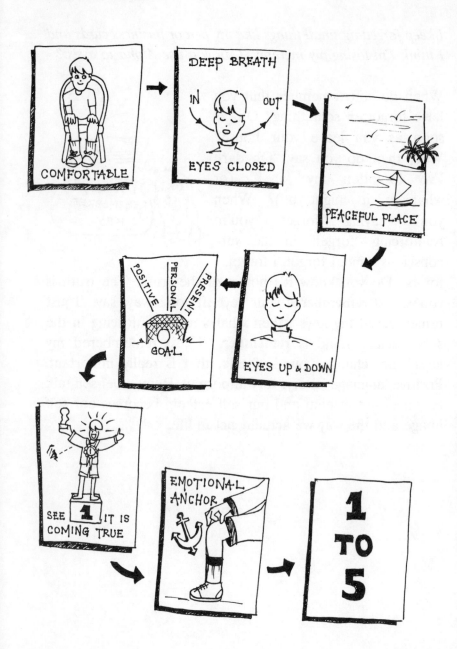

– TRUE MIND POWER –

Achieve Life Skills and Goals faster by using –

✦ *Positive Affirmation Statements*

with

✦ *Visualisation*

done in

✦ *Alpha — to communicate with the subconscious mind*

with

✦ *Emotion — the language of the subconscious mind*

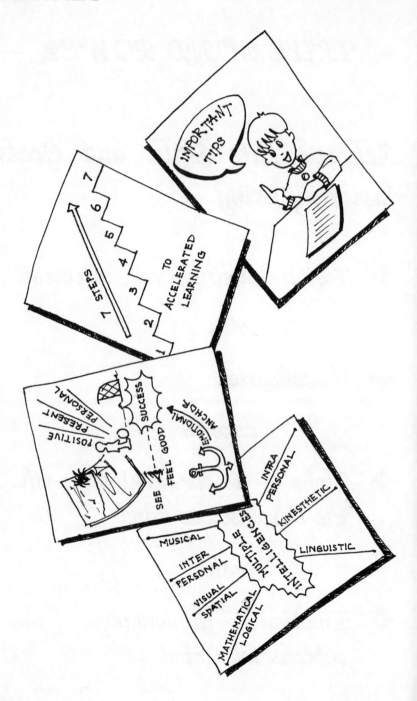

13

ACADEMIC ACCELERATED LEARNING

Purpose

The purpose of this chapter is to show how you can apply the tools and techniques, learned by doing the exercises in this book, to "academic" learning. Accelerated Learning techniques are being applied in schools, colleges, universities and corporations throughout the world. There is a quiet revolution going on which is designed to lift industrial age "schooling" to information age "education", and there are a number of books, reports and papers that have been written, principally by researchers. In Australia a number of schools and corporations embrace the concepts of "Accelerated Learning". Many trainers in Australia (national and international) use accelerated learning techniques in imparting their seminars and are active in expounding the principals of accelerated learning. Accelerated Learning Centres are operating for both the public and schools – it's a movement that is expanding.

I do not intend to present any of the growing evidence as to how accelerated learning techniques can triple learning rates (refer to the book *Accelerated Learning* by Colin Rose for this) however, I do intend to reiterate some techniques you may have already experienced as a result of reading this book, or indeed highlight techniques that you may not have experienced.

There are two extremely important requirements to engage in successful "accelerated learning":

✦ relaxation, and

✦ emotion.

I teach a way to successfully relax quickly and to use positive emotion in the "memory" process. The method is practical and easy and I believe unique. What I have to offer that sets me apart from other trainers is that I teach the "HOW" to relax and the "HOW" to use positive emotion. By reading this book and doing the exercises, or by attending my seminars, you can do the two most important things required to achieve accelerated learning.

The Theory of Multiple Intelligences

Howard Gardner published his theory of "Multiple Intelligences" in his book *Frames of Mind* in 1983. The accelerated learning movement widely embraces the concept, and indeed many educators and trainers use the theories either deliberately, as a result of Gardner's work, or naturally as a part of "naturally knowing" the techniques for good instruction.

I have been attending self awareness seminars for a considerable time and all the good ones use the intelligences to differing degrees. In fact I can recall learning at Duntroon Military Academy the "Theories and Practice of Good Instruction" which incorporated a number of the intelligences into the military training (as opposed to the academic training). My Sydney University training in Civil Engineering was not particularly noted for its "good instruction", nor did it incorporate many of the "Intelligences" researched by Gardner.

In my opinion, what Gardner has done with his work is "put the teachings of good instruction" firmly on the agenda within education per se. There is now no doubt that academics throughout the world are looking seriously at the different ways of learning so that there can be a high improvement on the "sit down, face the front, keep quiet and listen to me" attitude that I experienced.

A summary of the "multiple intelligences" and their application to a particular challenge follows: —

Intelligence	Application to a Particular Challenge
Mathematical/ Logical	Approach the problem logically, consider the aim, consider all aspects affecting that outcome, use comparisons, create sequences and charts and use systems. Work things out!
Visual/Spatial	Use colour, symbols and signs, illustrations and diagrams, prepare a

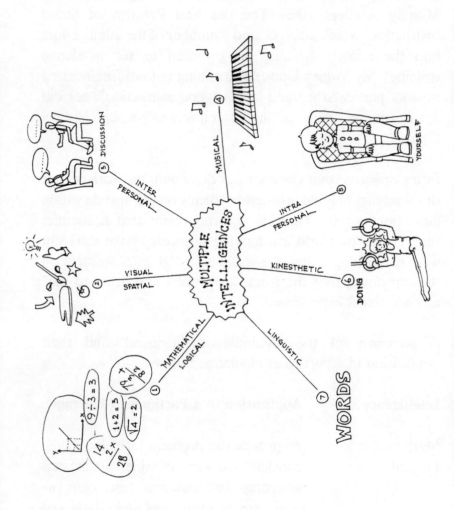

Mind Chart, list aspects that help to develop the total picture, use imaging to "see" the desired outcome. See the challenge and the solution.

Inter-personal

Use partners/mates/buddies to discuss the challenge, listen to others about their experiences with similar challenges, consider ethnic differences and other learning styles. Discuss the challenge and situation.

Musical

Use baroque music, at 56 to 64 beats per minute, whilst thinking about your challenges. Record the challenges with words over music or maybe make a song and play it to yourself.

Intra-personal

Sit quietly in Alpha and bring all aspects of the challenge into your mind. Ask yourself for a successful outcome, ask yourself next steps in solving the challenge, try the plan in your mind. Use your own personal power in a quiet meditative process.

Kinesthetic

Do anything that you can with the challenge, like: experiments, models, maps, diagrams, charts, graphs. Go for a walk or run and think about or discuss the challenge. Make up a play and act it out, especially the solution. The "doing"/"action" state sparks inventiveness and solutions.

Linguistic   Write the challenge, read it, tape record it and then listen to it — do this with all aspects of the challenge and the solution. Use words, explore proverbs, and metaphors, describe the challenge to yourself inside your mind in different ways, use symbols or mnemonics to describe it to yourself. Use words in every way you can.

Now to the most powerful process, which you have learned in this book:

Involve the subconscious mind (the memory) by: —

✦   **Relaxation** — go to your Peaceful Place

✦   **Goal Statement** — words framed in Positive, Present tense and Personal language

✦   **Imaging** — see the successful outcome and feel really good about it.

✦   **Emotionalise** — as you heighten your physical feelings, apply your Emotional Anchor.

Use this process to indelibly imprint your subconscious mind

with the outcome you want. What sort of intelligence is that?
The most powerful!

Seven Steps to Accelerated Learning

Step 1 — Relax

Use your Peaceful Place method of going into the Alpha
brain wave state. Inside your mind develop an interest in the
study/work you are about to do. Faking that interest is OK.

See yourself successfully using the information as a step to
whatever you wish to achieve. Play background baroque
music which is 56 to 64 beats per minute all the time (unless
you find it distracting).

Intelligences used are: Kinesthetic and Intra-personal. Note
— this can be done in a classroom situation.

213

Step 2 — Overview

Switch the brain on to the particular information by quickly

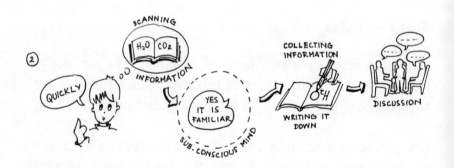

reviewing or scanning the information. The brain becomes more familiar with the information. Ask yourself questions as to what you want from this study session — if you're in a group ask each other. Write down your questions. Use quiet reflection.

Intelligences used are: Mathematical/logical, visual/spatial, inter and intra-personal and kinesthetic. Note — this can be done in a class room situation.

Step 3 — Initial Absorption

Generally this involves the absorption of logically or sequentially presented information. It could be by reading (for individual study) or say by lectures or seminars. For individual study, learn to read in the "accelerated learning" way and involve your creative brain by seeing (or imagine you're seeing) the words as pictures. Predominantly the initial information presented is by either visual or auditory presentation methods. However the challenge for all trainers

is to use all three modes — visual, auditory and kinesthetic presentation in any classroom or seminar situation. At the end of this step you must have a mind chart.

Intelligences used are: Visual/spatial and mathematical/logical (primarily). Note — these primary intelligences are used in most classroom situations — the challenge is to use more.

Step 4 — Processing the Information

In this process we need to expand the intelligences that we normally use. For individual work:

✦ Re-make Mind Charts and use pictures of scenes using the information

✦ Play baroque music (56 to 64 beats per minute) and describe your mind chart, recording both the music and your words, then play it back to yourself (Lazanov's passive learning technique)

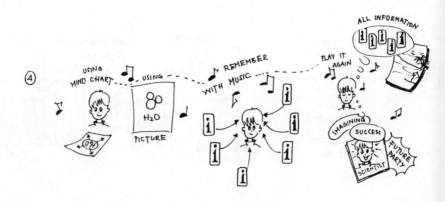

✦ Picture yourself in your Peaceful Place, using the information and imagining your future success by the application of that information. For instance, say you are to study mathematics as a first step towards your goal to be a Hotel Manager, what you do in your

Peaceful Place is to see yourself as a successful Hotel Manager — see yourself calculating the profitability and the occupancy rates, and imagine yourself using your mathematics to do this.

One of the most valuable ways of processing is by discussing the subject, and for all those individuals who struggle by themselves I suggest that you form discussion groups. In seminars or classroom situations most of the above processes can be used, plus the presenter has the advantage of using group dynamics so that learning can take place with a partner or a small group, with games, with role play, with a "future party" which is imaging that you have exactly what you want and acting it out in say a "cocktail party". You act out your success, pretending that the time period is ten years hence and that you have achieved everything you set out to achieve.

Intelligences used are: All seven. They can be used in classroom and seminar situations. For individuals, Inter-personal intelligence can not be used (this intelligence and the value of discussion is so important that you are encouraged to form study groups).

Step 5 — Memory Imprinting — with Emotion

To place the information into that part of your brain where you can recall easily, it is good to use a Mind Chart. This Mind Chart is like a picture with the information involving the creative side of the brain. So, look at the Mind Chart, go to your Peaceful Place, see or imagine you are seeing, the fact that you are confident and happy. See yourself recalling the information, maybe see yourself under pressure (say in an exam) recalling the information − see great results. Then feel really good about yourself with the new achievement and then use your Emotional Anchor.

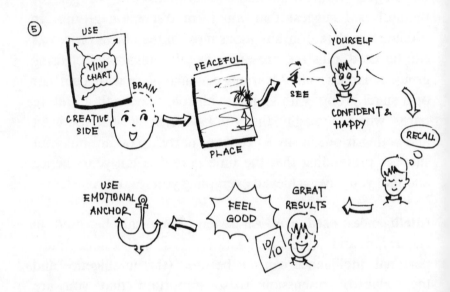

Intelligences used are: Visual/spatial, Intra-personal, kinesthetic and sometimes musical intelligences are used. Note − the most powerful resource is being relaxed and using emotion.

Step 6 − Use the Information

This involves practising with the information, rehearsing with it or writing about it. A most powerful way of using it is to discuss it. For individual learning, actually doing:

—   information exercises, say in discussion groups

—   old exam papers and answering questions, and

—   recreating mind charts and writing about the subject.

are the main actions to take.

Intelligences used are: Mathematical/logical, intra-personal, linguistic and kinesthetic. Note — for classrooms, inter-personal can be used to a great advantage.

Step 7 — Ongoing Review

A great way to achieve better recall is to look at your picture/your summary/your Mind Chart the next day, the next week, the next month and then the next year. As you look at it, go through the information in your mind, very quickly checking out what you do know and what you don't know. If you can place your Mind Chart on a wall in your study/ bedroom then do so — your peripheral vision always operates and takes note even when you're not conscious of

it. As often as you can go to your Peaceful Place and see yourself recalling the information (it's good to see yourself doing this under pressure — for instance at meetings or at an exam) and REMEMBER to feel really pleased with yourself.

Intelligences used are: Visual/spatial, intra-personal and kinesthetic. REMEMBER, the use of emotion in your Peaceful Place. For trainers and classroom situations it's great to have follow up/ review/ discussion times set aside for Step 7.

Summary of Important Tips

Learning Mode

Be aware of whether you are primarily a see-er, a listen-er or a do-er — it is most beneficial for you to use your primary mode. In my book *Students Steps to Success*, I explore this in more depth, with a couple of exercises to determine your primary mode — it's easy to do yourself. Do you use language like "I see what you mean" or "that rings a bell" or "I've got a grip on that")?

Subconscious Mind

Your subconscious mind is the storage house for all information. Memory is perfect in the subconscious mind; it is recall that we want. The Alpha state is the relaxed focused concentration state and it is the state in which we can communicate with the subconscious mind.

Interest

To create interest in the subject matter is essential for recall, that is, psych up and tell yourself that the subject matter is interesting and desirable to be known (remember, the subconscious mind does not know the difference between reality and imagination). Reward yourself (even if it's a jelly bean).

The Filter

The Filter of the Reticular Activating System lets in

information in which you are interested (so psych up before you study) and the filter opens up when you are relaxed (so relax and let the information go straight to the storage house — the subconscious mind).

Recall

Relax to recall (remember — breathe — it is the first step). When you are interested in the material you study and you are relaxed it goes to that part of the memory bank that can be easily accessed with recall. So to recall easily, study the material you are interested in, in the Alpha state (faking it till you make it — if necessary).

Exams

Set your goal for the exam. See yourself in your Peaceful Place, doing the exam. Feel great as you see the results of the exam and emotionalise it the way you have been taught. Your subconscious mind lets you be so confident when you actually do the exam and you do well by recalling all that you study.

Language

Remember to keep your self talk positive for this creates your self esteem and that self esteem goes to the subconscious mind which produces your self image. Choose to remember — even with your keys, brief case and the names of people you meet.

Doing it Does it

There is no substitute for this statement. You must just **DO IT** to achieve the skills and gain the 88% power in your subconscious mind.

Support

Enlist available support by referring to Appendix A on product information at the end of this book, page 230, and Appendix B on Support Mechanisms, page 238.

Summary of Steps to Achieve Accelerated Learning

1. Relax
2. Overview
3. Initial Absorption of Information
4. Processing the Information
5. Memory Imprinting with Emotion
6. Use the Information
7. Ongoing Review

Accelerated Learning is for All

From 0 to 5 years of age we all use accelerated learning naturally — remember the way we learned? It was fun, with a short attention span and it was in Alpha, when we learned more facts than it takes to get a university degree. We now know that the brain is the only organ in the body that when continually used and stimulated, will continue to develop. It is important to believe that when you get old or older your brain remains agile. Researchers throughout the world have shown that intelligence is not static, that when stimulated, it can continue to grow and be developed, and whilst this is not widely accepted, continued research, with continued proof, is having a positive effect on acceptance and belief in this research. It is significant that the Accelerated Learning movement world wide has embraced the concept that learning potential and intelligence are not static.

Twenty-Eight Ways

Twenty-eight Ways to Accelerate Life Skills in diagramatic form is shown on pages 226 to 227. When you study this Mind Chart you will remember and reactivate the whole of this book. Notice that the left hand side (page 226) is for Goals, and the right hand side (page 227) summarises Academic Skills.

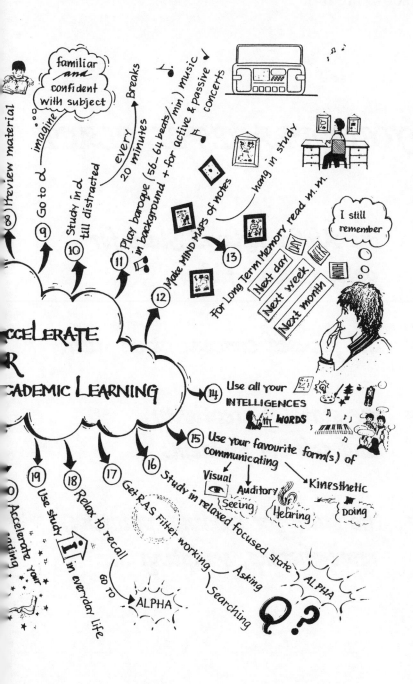

8) Preview material

9) Go to α

10) Study in α till distracted

familiar *and* confident with subject

imagine

11) Play baroque (56-64 beats/min) music in background + for active & passive concerts

every 20 minutes Breaks

12) Make MIND MAPS of notes

13) hang in study

For Long Term Memory read m.m.

Next day DAY
Next week WEEK
Next month

I still remember

ACCELERATE YOUR ACADEMIC LEARNING

14) Use all your INTELLIGENCES WORDS

15) Use your favourite form(s) of communicating

Visual — Seeing
Auditory — Hearing
Kinesthetic — Doing

16) Study in relaxed focused state
Get R.A.S. Filter working — Asking — Searching — ALPHA

17) Relax to recall GO TO ALPHA

18) Use study i in everyday life

19) Accelerate your reading

YOUR PEACEFUL PLACE

= *the Alpha Relaxed State for getting goals faster*

= *the focused concentration state*

= *the state of creativity and solving problems*

= *the state for reading, painting, remembering, sculpting ...*

EPILOGUE

I would like to leave you with one last example of how powerful the subconscious mind is.

In 1965 there was the documented death of a man dying of freezing to death. He accidentally locked himself in a freezer wagon in a rail yard in Maryland in the United States. It was on a Friday night, so he knew that no one was going to be able to return to the site for a couple of days. He had a marker pen so he thought that what he could do for mankind was to document his own death; what it was like to freeze to death; what happens to the human body. What it was like in his body after one hour, after two hours, and so on. How long would it take him to die by freezing? When his mates returned on Monday morning and opened up this particular van, it had writing all over the inside and their friend was dead on the floor. They then read the best documented evidence of what happens to a person when they freeze to death.

However what happened, and what you ought to know, is that the freezer van was not even turned on. The temperature inside that van was 56 degrees Fahrenheit (or 18 degrees Centigrade) all the time. The man's subconscious mind was told that the freezer van was on and that he was going to freeze death ... and he did. That's the power of the subconscious mind and how quickly and dramatically it can have an effect!

APPENDIX A - A PEACEFUL PLACE (PP) SERIES BOOKS, TAPES AND VIDEOS

A leap of consciousness is the most significant evolution which mankind is currently undergoing and I offer this information as an instrument towards accessing the power within you.

OTHER BOOKS BY SANDY:

Switch On to Your Inner Strength $20

Not until we're challenged by adversity do we experience our inner strength. This book is about how to use your inner strength, at any time, to enhance your peace and power.

No Need for Heroes $20

A true story about the Engineer Troop commanded by Sandy in Vietnam 1965-66. These original "Tunnel Rats" give hair raising and hilarious accounts of their adventures.

Students Steps to Success $25

Designed as a work book for students over 13 years or supportive parents, which imparts empowering life skills and accelerated academic learning techniques. This book has been acclaimed by professors, teachers and principals.

PEACEFUL PLACE (PP) TAPES:

In all my meditative tapes I have used the wonderful inspirational music by **Ken Davis.**

PP No. 1: Instrumental $20

Relaxation, study and inner peace. The music *Infinite Joy* created by Ken Davis especially for Sandy MacGregor.

PP No. 2: Guided Imagery $20

Guided Imagery is used to create and reinforce your Peaceful Place and your Emotional Anchor. Porpoising and putting it all together to achieve your goals faster is included. Sandy does the guided imagery over *Infinite Joy*.

Any three tapes from PP Tapes Numbers 3 to 15   **$45**

PP No. 3 — Releasing Hurt   **$18**
This meditation is spoken over *Endless Emotion* from *Crystal Clear*. Pain is a signal for the body that there is something out of balance. It sometimes serves as a warning (for example the imminent birth of a baby) and what you can often do is to release the intensity of the hurt in the pain.

PP No. 4 — Healing Yourself   **$18**
This meditation is spoken over *Our World* from *Pan Flutes with Nature*. Using guided imagery and your own visualisation you work towards attacking your illness by directing your mind and activating your own immune system. Remember this technique is to be used in combination with others including having faith in your doctor, your treatment, yourself and your spiritual faith, whatever is true for you.

PP No. 5 — Meditation   **$18**
This meditation is spoken over *Celestial Journey*. The meditation helps to relax and release stress at deep levels by concentrating on breathing. If you prefer to use it for spiritual growth, you can actively, silently or aloud, chant names of God eg. "Hu", "Ohm" or perhaps "Love" or "Peace".

PP No. 6 — Forgiveness   **$18**
This meditation is spoken over *Early Morning in the Rain Forest*. Forgiveness is such an important element of daily living. Coming to terms with yourself and others in areas such as judgements, anger, resentment, guilt or blame is a key to your own progress.

PP No 7 — Tapping Your Creativity   **$18**
This meditation is spoken over *Soaring* from *Pan Flutes with Nature*. Your own creativity can be accessed for it resides in

your subconscious mind. You can use it for solving problems (as did Einstein) or for inventions (as did Edison) or for writing, poetry, sculpture, art, painting, etc. (as did Salvador Dali). It's exciting!

PP No. 8 — Weight Release $18
This meditation is spoken over *Fly Like a Bird* from *Atmospheres*. What do you want to do when you lose something? That's right — find it again! Hence the term "weight release". This tape works with your goal, changing habits, increasing your metabolic rate and a quick way to stop eating between meals — all without stress.

PP No. 9 — Letting Go Anger $18
This meditation is spoken over *Calling You* from *Crystal Clear*. Anger involves aspects relating to resentment, guilt, blame or judgements — of self, or others. Acceptance is a great way forward and your own self esteem just grows.

PP No. 10 — Self Worth and Confidence $18
This meditation is spoken over *I'm in Heaven* from *Love*. It's great to know that you are a truly wonderful, special person; that you are worthy and that your confidence grows and grows. One of the biggest keys is unconditional love.

PP No. 11 — Achieving in Exams and Effective Study $18
This meditation is spoken over *Radiance* from *Atmospheres*. Wonderful, practical hints for achieving more, without stress, by using your subconscious mind. Gain clarity and focus both in exams and whilst studying.

PP No. 12 — Making Sleep Easy and Useful $18
This meditation is spoken over *Blissful Sleep*. You spend one third of your life sleeping (or trying to sleep). This tape shows you how to achieve an easy, restful sleep .... and to make it useful, by first clearing your mind of all the day's activities .... and then by using your subconscious mind to help you

succeed in whatever is happening the following day.

PP No. 13 — Inner Peace and Harmony $18

This meditation is spoken over *Dreaming of Angels* from *Pan Flutes Over The Ocean*. My experience of inner peace was to work through, during meditation, acceptance and cooperation; secondly to have unconditional love of self and others and then to apply a process of forgiveness. All our journeys are different and I'm sure these techniques will assist.

PP No. 14 — Improving Relationships $18

This meditation is spoken over *Dreaming of Angels* from *Pan Flutes by the Ocean*. "To be the person that I would like to spend the rest of my life with" is where your relationship starts. This tape has a number of powerful exercises on it which guide you through knowing what you want, and then demonstrating that in your life. Why? Because what you give out, you get back.

PP No. 15 — Overcoming Fear $18

This meditation is spoken over *More than a Friend* from *Pan Flutes by the Ocean*. Know that you are greater than any debilitating thought. This tape teaches a process of observing your thoughts, letting them go, and implanting into the subconscious mind success in conquering any debilitating thought or fear. It's wonderful relaxation too.

Instructions for Use

Essentially you need to choose a quiet comfortable place where you will not sleep. Play Side 1 first and then Side 2 as many times as you need to (at least twice a day). My advice is to keep the tape for personal use.

PACKS:

Piece of Mind Pack $50

Sandy's **Book** *Piece of Mind* and **Tapes** — PP No.1 —

Relaxation, study and inner peace. The music *Infinite Joy* created by Ken Davis, and **PP No. 2** — Guided imagery is used to create and reinforce your Peaceful Place and your Emotional Anchor. Porpoising and putting it all together to achieve your goals faster is included. Sandy does the Guided Imagery over *Infinite Joy*.

Audio Pack for *Students Steps to Success* Book $35

This economic pack includes: *A Peaceful Place No. 2 — Guided Imagery; A Peaceful Place No. 10 — Self Worth and Confidence* and *A Peaceful Place No. 11 — Achieving in Exams and Effective Study.*

The Peaceful Place Collection $149

There are 8 one-hour audio tapes in this collection. One tape is baroque classics and the remainder are guided imagery. Both sides of a *Peaceful Place No. 3* is one tape whilst the remainder are Side 2 only of a *Peaceful Place Nos. 4 to 15.* (Refer to the above titles).

Tapes (2): Accelerated Learning Music $35

A selection of Baroque Classics all having a timing of between 56 and 64 beats per minute. Science has now shown that our heartbeat tends to get in time with the music and thus we in turn relax and reach the Alpha brainwave state. That's why this music is good for meditation and releasing stress, accelerated learning techniques such as Lazanov's Passive Concert, and for guided imagery and creativity. Use it as background music for studying — from mathematics to languages, or at work. Relaxation increases productivity.

CD — THE GIFT OF RELAXATION: $25

With the guided imagery you build a Peaceful Place and then using the colours you go to a deeper meditation state; the CD finishes with thirty minutes of Infinite Joy. The CD can be used for relaxation, meditation, creativity, sleep, etc.

THE CALM KIT: $195

The Calm Kit is the CALM Life Skills Seminar — on video, audio and book. With the CALM KIT you will get powerful tools and techniques to use the power of the subconscious mind to relax in 30 seconds, reduce stress, improve memory, sleep deeper, release weight, stop smoking, improve confidence, pass exams, improve sports performance ...

Contents of the Calm Kit: Videos (1 hour each)

Video No. 1 — How to Use the Power of Your Minds.
In the first half of this video Sandy describes his personal journey and experiences in becoming aware of how to use the power of the subconscious mind.

The second half provides an educational perspective into its use, including:

1. Practical demonstrations of using your subconscious power.

2. The science of the mind — Left/Right, Mind Charting, The RAS Filter, language of the subconscious mind and four different brain wave states.

3. Proof and demonstration of Alpha waves using technology — the IBVA and the Alpha trainer.

4. Testimonials.

5. An overview of seminars, books and tapes.

Video No. 2 — Highlights of the CALM Life Skills Seminar

Actual seminar highlights edited to show, teach and revise powerful mind techniques.

Audio Tapes

A PP No. 2 — Guided Imagery — Building Your Peaceful Place, Relaxing in 30 Seconds, Your Emotional Anchor and Goals.

Three Audio tapes you can use in your car for empowering techniques:

Tape A: Side 1 — The Science of the Mind
　　　　　Side 2 — Introduction of CALM Concepts
Tape B: Side 1 — Discussing Alpha and Using Emotion
　　　　　Side 2 — Goals, WIIFMs and Visualisation
Tape C: Side 1 — 8 Steps to Achieving Goals Faster
　　　　　Side 2 — 7 Steps to Accelerate Your Learning

Book

The Australasian Best Seller *Piece of Mind* showing how to switch on to the 88% power in your subconscious mind, in 30 seconds, to relax and release stress, accelerate learning and to achieve goals faster.

VIDEO TAPE:

How to Use the Power of Your Minds　　　　　　　　**$50**

Please refer to the description of Video No. 1 in the CALM KIT for this Video Tape.

FOR ORDERS:	AUSTRALIA	NEW ZEALAND
PLEASE PHONE:	**(02)439 7188**	**(03) 382 2400**
OR FAX:	**(02)439 7587**	**(03) 382 2401**
E MAIL	**calm@ozemail.com.au**	

PLEASE NOTE, PRICES ARE IN AUSTRALIAN DOLLARS

APPENDIX B — CALM SEMINARS
(Creative Accelerated Learning Methods)

We have a team of qualified facilitators throughout Australia who conduct the following seminars:

LIFE SKILLS (Two Days):
First Day:

❖ How to release stress and relax in a few seconds (for insomnia, anxiety, arguments).

❖ Accelerated learning (memory, recall, exams, concentration).

❖ Achieving goals faster (eg. releasing weight, sleeping easier, increasing confidence or sales, etc.)

Second Day: working with the mind at deeper levels to —

❖ Take control over your own body.

❖ Relieve pain and take the first steps to healing yourself.

❖ Obtain the deeper meditative state.

❖ Tap your creativity.

CHI — Creating Happiness Intentionally

This is a four day live-in seminar for which the pre-qualification is the two-day Life Skills Seminar. CHI is about getting on track with your life and using mind techniques to decide:

❖ What is your life's purpose now?

❖ What are goals to support your life's purpose?

❖ What are your values to support your goals?

❖ How do you change your values or goals to support your life's purpose?

TTT — Train the Trainer for CALM Seminars

This is a six-day live-in seminar for those who wish to teach the seminars. Pre-qualifications to attend TTT include CALM Life Skills Seminar, CHI Seminar, Enthusiasm, Interest and

Selection. Prior to working as a qualified trainer there is a requirement to work with qualified trainers over 6 to 8 CALM Life Skills Seminars.

CHILDREN'S — Groups 6-9 and 10-13 years
Among techniques taught are:
- ❖ The ability to relax and its application to improving life skills
- ❖ Exercises designed to assist whole brain learning
- ❖ Increasing self confidence and self esteem.

STUDENT SUCCESS — 14-18 years
The key outcomes include:
- ❖ Learn lifelong skills to increase confidence and self esteem.
- ❖ Learn methods to handle the challenge of change.
- ❖ Effectively deal with all study and exam stress.
- ❖ Learn efficient life skills goal setting techniques.

STUDENTS IN SCHOOLS
This seminar is similar to Student Success (above), however they can be tailored to suit individual school demands.

CORPORATE
In the main they are two-day seminars which can be done in four sessions of 3 hours, tailored to suit the client, with agreed outcomes. The range includes:
- ❖ Achieving With Managing and Releasing Stress
- ❖ Strengthening Organisational Change
- ❖ Achieving Goals Faster
- ❖ First Steps to Enhancing Skills Development
- ❖ Foundations of Team Building
- ❖ The Precursor to Maximising Customer Service

SUPPORT MECHANISMS
We believe that it is important for a personal development company to be able to offer ongoing support to participants.

We do this in various ways: —

- ❖ Telephone support
- ❖ Regular Follow-up evenings
- ❖ Repeat privileges for those who do the seminars
- ❖ Two-hour Active Meditation Seminars which serve as an introduction for friends or for reinforcement for the Life Skill Seminar participants
- ❖ **Free Newsletter** for one year for seminar participants and thereafter $10 per year (open to non participants of seminars).

FOR MORE INFORMATION ABOUT PRODUCTS OR SEMINARS

AUSTRALIA: **CALM CENTRE**
2nd Level
80 Chandos Street
Crows Nest NSW 2065

Internet Home Page — www.lightenup.com.au/calm

TELEPHONE:	**(02) 439 7188**
FAX:	**(02) 439 7587**
TOLL FREE:	**016 280 344**
E MAIL	**calm@ozemail.com.au**

NEW ZEALAND: ACCELERATED LEARNING ASSOCIATES
PO Box 24-123
Christchurch 6, New Zealand

TELEPHONE:	**(03) 382 2400**
FAX:	**(03) 382 2401**

SWITCH ON
TO YOUR INNER STRENGTH

**Here are some extracts of personal stories
from Sandy's latest book** *Switch on to Your Inner Strength*

Julie Van den Driesen from Victoria stopped smoking with no fuss. Then she proceeded to release 5 stone (31 kilos).

Reg Wells from Western Australia couldn't walk properly 3 weeks prior to running a marathon. He reached inside and achieved his goal.

Ariane Halls from New South Wales is 12 years old. She gained 4 scholarships to high school and achieved her swimming and athletic goals.

Kieran John Forde from New South Wales coped with the diverse demands of life's challenges — stress, confidence, relationships, and finance.

Wendy Burbury from Tasmania went inside to make a big decision — yes, she would have a mastectomy.

I continually use Sandy's PP techniques in many ways, but primarily in my cue sport (eightball) and health. After winning local competitions, a great highlight for me was to beat Eddie Charlton in a best of three matches in December 1992. I beat him 2 to nil and have his autographed cue and video of the matches to prove it! I told everyone I would beat the world champion and current Australian Champion and said "I could see his cue on my wall". That's there, and now there's another. In February 1994 I had a rematch with Eddie and was lucky enough to win for a second time against him, 2/1. This was an important match as it proved the first win was not just luck. I won the first game and Eddie the second. In the last game Eddie broke the balls and then I potted all 7 coloured balls and the black in a row to win.

Glenn Connor, Victoria

A note from Sandy: Glenn is truly inspirational — despite being confined to a wheelchair following a serious motorcycle accident 14 years ago when he was 17 years old he has competed and triumphed against some of the best pool, snooker, eightball and nineball players in Australia.

I am writing to tell you about some of the wonderful experiences I have had using techniques you taught me at your CALM seminar. Since doing the Seminar I have been practising my PP and I really got the opportunity to test it out when I discovered I had to have some extensive dental treatment.

Since I was a child I have always been terrified of dental visits and the worst moment for me was always seeing and feeling the needle. As I child I used to regularly faint when having injections! This time however, during the first visit for treatment, before the injection, I went to my PP, which I can now do very quickly, and my mind went somewhere else. Almost straight away I was in Alpha state and I felt totally relaxed and happy, even during the injection, and right through the treatment. Even though a part of my mind was conscious of the fact I was at the dentist, I was not experiencing any anxiety.

*I had to go for many subsequent visits and each time I practised my PP, sometimes going into a deeper meditation. I couldn't believe it — I was actually **enjoying** going to the dentist! My dentist was pleasantly surprised too.*

Lindsay Roy, New South Wales

    I represented Australia in plumbing in the recent Skills Olympics in Taiwan. My goal was to win a Gold Medal. I did heaps of practice and constantly visualised the success of my goal. The competition is over 4 long days and my major disadvantage was to work with unfamiliar pipe sizes and a pipe bending machine — ones I had never used before but with which competitors from the Asian countries were familiar. I didn't know that this was to be the case, so you can imagine how "down" I felt when I was told this news. I got the BRONZE Medal (only missing out on Gold by less than 1%), and got the GOLD medal for the highest points of any Australian competing throughout the 35 trades. I constantly used a specially focused meditation tape which Sandy prepared for me, working hard in the meditation and Alpha state for 3 months beforehand. I prepared myself mentally to get a Gold Medal, to sleep soundly every night of the competition and to manage stress.

Jason Freund, New South Wales

In 1990 I was advised that doing my Higher School Certificate was probably not in my best interest, as I should not, and really could not expect to receive over 40 as a TER. The truth is, I had nothing wrong with me, no crippling disease or brain disorder, but more, that talent of being dyslexic, and this is where Sandy helped me.

After completing Sandy's CALM Seminar in 1991 I learned that being dyslexic was a gift I had been given. There were of course the frustrations of being 18 years old with a reading and spelling capacity of an 11 year old. This, coupled with an extremely high IQ, tremendous determination and dedication, made learning a challenging experience.

By applying techniques learned from Sandy I found myself in the top 10 in all subjects. Not only was my school work dramatically improving, but I also increased my interest in Stage Management, where by the end of 1992 I had managed 10 professional and school productions. My chronic asthma was controlled, not through large doses of medication, but by intense meditation.

In 1992 I set myself targets and goals in regard to my Higher School Certificate. I quickly learnt that setting goals is one thing, but doing them is another.

CALM taught me to take control of my life and "Seize the day". In January 1993 I received my Higher School Certificate results. I had visualised the whole experience from the opening of the envelope, my excitement, my parents expressions of delight. Sometimes all the visualisations can not get you prepared for the actual event.

The event was as I visualised, but far more. In all my subjects I was in the top 10% of the state, as well as being placed 5th in the state for Modern History.

I set my goals, I worked towards them and the best part is I out-did them. CALM has allowed me to turn a negative into a positive, believe in myself, set goals and out-do them, but most of all I have learned "the sky is the limit".

Thanks Sandy and may all the success in the world come to you.

Georgina Bovill, New South Wales

*Sandy, I received your pack of **"Piece of Mind"** book and two tapes
in October 1995. If you had told me I could instantly gain noticeable
improvement in one day I would not have believed you. I must also be a
left-brained sceptic. I have been wallowing in despair for six years. I've read
many self-help books and I could not rid myself of that constant feeling of
dread, nor could I sleep at night. It took Sandy MacGregor to show me how
to help myself. Since using the techniques I have now slept 7 to 8 hours every
night. I've had interruptions to my sleep, eg. late night 'phone calls, storms
with thunder and lightening and still have been able to return to sleep easily.*

*Furthermore, I have just returned from Canada and USA. In years
gone by I have needed to take a Rohypnol sleeping tablet on these journeys.
This time I slept for 7 hours during the flight over, and on the way back,
with no drugs.*

Kevin Gray, Victoria

PHOTOCOPY THIS PRODUCT ORDER FORM

CALM Pty Ltd PO Box 482 Lindfield NSW 2070
Ph: (02) 439 7188 Fax: (02)439 7587

Name: ....

Address: .... Town/Suburb:..........................

P/Code:.................... Telephone: (Wk)............................(H)..............

	Unit Price	Total $
BOOK: *Switch On To Your Inner Strength*	$20	....
BOOK: *No Need for Heroes*	$20	....
BOOK: *Students' Steps to Success*	$25	....
AUDIO TAPES (2): STUDENTS' STEPS TO SUCCESS	$35	....
BOOK: *Piece of Mind*	$20	....
AUDIO TAPE: PP No 1: INSTRUMENTAL	$20	....
AUDIO TAPE: PP No 2: GUIDED IMAGERY	$20	....
PACK: *Piece of Mind* AND PP No 1 and No 2	$50	....
CALM KIT: *POM* Book, Tapes & Video	$195	....
AUDIO TAPES (2): ACCEL. LEARNING MUSIC	$35	....
CD: THE GIFT OF RELAXATION	$25	....
VIDEO: HOW TO USE THE POWER OF YOUR MINDS	$50	....
AUDIO TAPES (8): PP C'TION(PP 3-15+A/L Music)	$149	....

ANY 3 PP MEDITATION TAPES ✓ ☐ below $45   ....

		Unit Price	Total $
PP No 3:	RELEASING HURT	☐ $18	....
PP No 4:	HEALING YOURSELF	☐ $18	....
PP No 5:	MEDITATION	☐ $18	....
PP No 6:	FORGIVENESS	☐ $18	....
PP No 7:	TAPPING YOUR CREATIVITY	☐ $18	....
PP No 8:	WEIGHT RELEASE	☐ $18	....
PP No 9:	LETTING GO ANGER	☐ $18	....
PP No 10:	SELF WORTH AND CONFIDENCE	☐ $18	....
PP No 11:	ACHIEVE IN EXAMS & EFFECT. STUDY	☐ $18	....
PP No 12:	MAKING SLEEP EASY AND USEFUL	☐ $18	....
PP No 13:	INNER PEACE AND HARMONY	☐ $18	....
PP No 14:	IMPROVING RELATIONSHIPS	☐ $18	....
PP No 15:	OVERCOMING FEAR	☐ $18	....

PACKAGING & POST COST ($4.00)   **$ 4.00**

TOTAL: $_____

PAYMENT DETAILS (Please tick ☑)

☐ Cheque   ☐ B/C   ☐ Visa   ☐ M/C   ☐ Money Order

☐☐☐☐ ☐☐☐☐ ☐☐☐☐ ☐☐☐☐

Card Member's A/C Name: ....

ExpiryDate:............................ Signature:..................................

WHAT MOVED ME TO DO THIS WORK

Here is my personal story. I share it with you because it demonstrates why I "walk my talk" using this technique. When you see how a "prove-it-to-me", professional and military person such as myself witnessed so clearly the power of our minds .... you may be more able to see the power you have just waiting to be tapped ....

On 23rd January 1987 my life was a happy one. I was the father of six children, a retired Army Colonel decorated in the Vietnam War with a Military Cross for bravery in tunnel conflicts, and a Civil Engineer. I had a bright future.

And then tragedy struck in a seemingly senseless way. My three daughters were gunned down and killed in their Sydney home by an intruder. I went to the brink of mental devastation.

I then found what human spirit is all about. This crisis made me a witness to the true power of our minds. By using a powerful mind technique, I saved my life from becoming one of hatred and self pity.

I was able to come to terms with the death of my three daughters .... and I found that when I was "stressed out", I could literally release that stress in 30 seconds. Thankfully, I had developed this skill before the crisis.

I started investigating this technique in 1981 when my eldest son, Andrew, was using it to control his asthma attacks. The profound power of it was demonstrated when Andrew was in an accident. He used this technique to save his badly broken leg from amputation.

Using the same technique, I released 22 kilograms. I went on to find that I could triple my learning rate, take on new challenges without stress, and switch focus of my concentration in 30 seconds. I then taught my two younger children the techniques which they then used to read between 600 and 800 words a minute, touch type at 35 to 50 words per minute and to release hurt, gain confidence, and lots more.

This technique is powerful in both your personal and business life.

Over the years I've had so much experience with witnessing the proof and power of this technique, I feel it's my **responsibility to teach how to develop this crucial life skill**. To this end, I have written three other books:

❖ *Switch On to Your Inner Strength* — We've all got it! It's about how to tap and use your Inner Strength.

❖ *No Need for Heroes* — Vietnam experiences with the Foreword by Lt General John Sanderson, Chief of the General Staff

❖ *Students Steps to Success* — Foreword by Associate Professor David Smith, Faculty of Education, University of Sydney.

I now run a company dedicated to assisting others to access the power within them. Together with my Trainers, we present to the Public, Educational and Corporate Sectors. My seminars, books, tapes and videos teach about the application of the power of the subconscious mind, using scientific facts (**replacing hype with proof**) in a very experiential way, showing *how* to harness the power of your mind, step by step .... so you'll have it "on tap" forever.